Adam Lent is the European Director of Innovation at Ashoka – the global network of over 3,000 leading social innovators and entrepreneurs. Previously he was Head of Economics for the UK Trades Union Congress, Director of the RSA Action and Research Centre and a Research Fellow in the Department of Politics at Sheffield University. He is the author of *British Social Movements Since 1945: Sex, Colour, Peace and Power* (Palgrave Macmillan, 2002).

Small is Powerful

WHY THE ERA OF BIG BUSINESS,
BIG GOVERNMENT AND BIG CULTURE
IS OVER

Adam Lent

unbound

unbound

This edition first published in 2016

Unbound
6th Floor Mutual House 70 Conduit Street London W1S 2GF
www.unbound.co.uk

Text Design by Ellipsis Digital Ltd, Glasgow

Grateful Acknowledgements:
Miles Corak (2012), milescorak.com

A CIP record for this book is available from the British Library

ISBN 978-1-78352-121-0 (trade paperback)
ISBN 978-1-78352-123-4 (ebook)
ISBN 978-1-78352-122-7 (limited edition)

Printed in Great Britain by Clays Ltd, St Ives Plc

1 3 5 7 9 8 6 4 2

For my small but powerful family:
Laura, Talia and Sahana

With special thanks to
Ian and Caroline Laing

Dear Reader,

The book you are holding came about in a rather different way to most others. It was funded directly by readers through a new website: Unbound. Unbound is the creation of three writers. We started the company because we believed there had to be a better deal for both writers and readers. On the Unbound website, authors share the ideas for the books they want to write directly with readers. If enough of you support the book by pledging for it in advance, we produce a beautifully bound special subscribers' edition and distribute a regular edition and e-book wherever books are sold, in shops and online.

This new way of publishing is actually a very old idea (Samuel Johnson funded his dictionary this way). We're just using the internet to build each writer a network of patrons. Here, at the back of this book, you'll find the names of all the people who made it happen.

Publishing in this way means readers are no longer just passive consumers of the books they buy, and authors are free to write the books they really want. They get a much fairer return too – half the profits their books generate, rather than a tiny percentage of the cover price.

If you're not yet a subscriber, we hope that you'll want to join our publishing revolution and have your name listed in one of our books in the future. To get you started, here is a £5 discount on your first pledge. Just visit unbound.com, make your pledge and type **smallpower** in the promo code box when you check out.

Thank you for your support,

Dan, Justin and John
Founders, Unbound

Contents

Small is Powerful

Acknowledgements

First and foremost, my deepest thanks go to all those who saw fit to pledge money towards the publication of *Small is Powerful*. Without you, this book would not have happened. I hope you feel I have lived up, at least partially, to your expectations.

Many more have contributed in other ways. Particular thanks must go to Ben Dellot, Max Yoshioka and Chris Thoung who conducted research with me for publications by The Royal Society of the Arts (RSA), which has informed sections of the book. The RSA has also been very kind in allowing me to reproduce short revised extracts from my 2012 paper *Generation Enterprise*, which appear in Chapters 2 and 12.

Others have been incredibly generous with their time in talking through the ideas and commenting on drafts. I would like to give a special mention to Anthony Painter whose wise counsel and open mind proved the perfect antidote to my authorial neuroses. He has played a big part in helping me develop the key themes here. The following are also due thanks for their comments and thoughts: Jason Bade, Scott Bade, Katy Evans, Alex Fox, Ross Hall, Catherine Howe, Matt Lent, Jolyon Maugham, Oliver Reichardt, Gerald Rothman, Clifford Singer, Graham Smith and Stuart White. Luke Johnson, in particular, has been incredibly generous in his support and advice and I am delighted that he has written the Foreword.

The team at Unbound has helped me enormously through the not entirely untraumatic process of crowdfunding. They have also provided incredibly wise advice and enthusiasm throughout the writing and publication phases. A particularly honourable mention must go to Xander Cansell who has borne my delays and interminable questions with saintly patience.

I also owe a debt of gratitude to the late E.F. Schumacher. I reread *Small is Beautiful* while on holiday and around 20 years after my first reading. I certainly didn't agree with it all and I doubt very much that, if he were still alive, he would agree with all of my book. No doubt I would be upbraided for ignoring environmental concerns, which results from my lack of expertise in that area rather than any lack of concern for that important challenge. But Schumacher's vision of a world where resources, technology and power are distributed widely enough to allow everyone to achieve their creative potential has been a major source of inspiration for the ideas developed here. For that reason I have entitled my book in honour of his classic without any claim to equivalence in quality or insight.

Many other authors have been both an inspiration and important sources for the contents of the book. This work does not pretend to be an academic text but a readable and accessible argument for change. For that reason I have not followed academic conventions of referencing and citation but all of the authors and works that have contributed to the book are mentioned either in the text, footnotes or in the reading lists at the end of the book which are sorted by chapter.

Finally, my deepest thanks go to my wife, Laura Sukhnandan, who has not only offered incisive and occasionally merciless comments on earlier drafts but has been a patient source of encouragement and practical support. As I have discovered, crowdfunding and writing a book is not for the faint hearted so I have been fortunate to have someone so stout of heart at my side.

Foreword

I first met Adam Lent when I chaired the Royal Society of Arts (RSA) and he was working there in charge of research. He produced fascinating new insights into the growth of self-employment in Britain and saw that a majority of those who start a business or become a freelancer do so principally because they want more freedom and independence. I have been obsessed for decades with the rise of entrepreneurship in our country and how it is changing our economy and society. Work is not being created by the government or large corporations: almost all new jobs are being generated by smaller, newer companies and an army of freelancers. We need to understand and embrace this phenomenon and help those who start new enterprises of all sorts to thrive.

Adam Lent has written a manifesto for citizens who want to control their own destiny. This book is a fascinating blend of history, economics and philosophy that cannot easily be defined using traditional political labels, and I hope it catches the attention of those across the political spectrum. Though Lent comes from a broadly left-wing background, he has studied the works of economists like von Mises, Schumpeter, Hayek and McCloskey, and he understands their merits. He notes that the left's embrace of big government leads to an unhealthy concentration of power, bureaucracy, waste, distorted incentives and overall impoverishment. Top-down, centralised public service and welfare models do not work in the 21st century. Today's voters demand choice, diversity and efficiency from the state, rather than politicians held hostage by vested interests like unions or big business.

New technologies are enabling populations to run their own lives without the suffocating influence of institutions, which means that sheer size is no longer an overwhelming advantage in many commercial matters. Economies of scale don't act as huge barriers to entry in the way they once did. Disruptive new firms are challenging the old oligopolies across an ever-expanding array of industries – from the media to supermarkets to banking and beyond. In many sectors, like brewing and utilities, there are defensive mergers leading to ever-greater concentration among the monoliths. But I think these lumbering giants will still lose share and dominance. In many sectors it is cheaper than ever for upstarts to enter, and consumers are no longer as loyal to mega-brands and faceless corporations as they once were.

I have spent my career working in smaller, dynamic companies: I could not bear the idea of working for a faceless multinational, infested with office politics and mainly concerned with managing decline. I hope in the years to come such monstrosities are broken up and that hundreds of more agile, innovative offshoots spring up instead. Books like *Small is Powerful* help to encourage these trends by reminding readers that they do have the wherewithal to determine their own future.

While I do not wholly agree with all of Adam Lent's proposals and the various views he puts forward in this book, I think it is an important addition to a vital debate. I hope it is widely read and discussed and perhaps even stimulates changes in the way society is organised. We should be excited by possibilities offered by the future rather than be prisoners of the past.

Luke Johnson
Entrepreneur and Columnist for the *Sunday Times*, 2016

Section I

WHY SMALL IS POWERFUL

1

Defying Gravity

Never before or since was a sausage so revolutionary. On 9 March 1522, a Swiss entrepreneur in the new and subversive world of printing invited 12 people over for dinner.

At his Zurich home, Christoph Froschauer, sliced some delicious Swiss Fasnachtskiechli and handed it around to his assembled friends. Not much of a meal maybe but enough to inspire a revolution across Europe.

That day happened to be the first Sunday of Lent, the period when Christians atone for their sins by making a personal sacrifice of some kind. As had been the case for many centuries, the Catholic Church had ruled on what those sacrifices should be. One of the most revered by Christians, the great majority of whom belonged to the Catholic Church, was eating no meat over the Lenten period.

Froschauer's carnivorous dinner was a deliberate flouting of this rule. It was a thumbing of the nose in a public and calculated way to the Catholic hierarchy. But what made the event a spark for rebellion across Europe was the presence of a notorious priest.

That priest was Huldrych Zwingli and he had a reputation for challenging many of the core features of the Catholic Church in his weekly sermons. Most famously, he had attacked the idea that the compulsory taxes the Church imposed on its parishioners were divinely sanctioned.

But it was a horrific outbreak of bubonic plague, which killed at least one quarter of the city's population, that elevated Zwingli from noisy rebel to living saint. Unlike many other well-off and well-connected individuals, the priest not only stayed in the city but also continued his pastoral duties administering to the sick and dying at a time of unimaginable fear and grief. Inevitably, he contracted the disease and despite the deeply unpleasant symptoms, he managed to compose three celebrated and lengthy poems on illness, death and recovery.

So a legend and a hero to the people of one of the wealthiest cities in Europe was endorsing Froschauer's deliberate mischief.

The controversy only deepened when Zwingli gave a sermon defending the dinner. His argument was simple but subversive. He claimed that the only law to which a Christian had to submit was that ordained by the word of God as given in the Bible. As there was nothing in either the Old or the New Testament forbidding the eating of flesh during Lent, a Christian should make their own choice about whether they did or did not consume meat.

Not only was he actively disagreeing with the views of the Church leadership, he was positing the notion that beyond the word of the Bible, individuals should have the freedom to make their own decisions about how they practised their faith. This challenged the very notion that any human hierarchy could make pronouncements with the authority of God behind them.

Zwingli's rebellion added momentum to a similar uprising in Germany led by Martin Luther. It then rapidly spread throughout Europe. This "Reformation" was the first continent wide uprising against the most – and arguably the only

– significant hierarchical, centralised organisation of the time.

It proved to be a rebellion of such force that it ignited a struggle that has lasted to this day. On the one side of this struggle are those who believe in a world shaped by the millions of diverse and free decisions of individuals, families and small organisations – what I refer to in this book as *small power*. On the other are those who favour a world dominated by a handful of big, hierarchical institutions and their narrow range of values – or *big power*.

A HISTORY OF BIG VERSUS SMALL: THE VERY SHORT VERSION

Part of this book explores the history of this battle between big and small power. It reveals how despite the power of Zwingli and Luther's uprising, big power fought back and re-established itself in the form of the absolute monarchies of the 17th and 18th centuries.

With freedom stifled in Europe, the flame of small power could only be kept alive in distant American colonies. There the principles behind the uprising against the Catholic Church became much more developed and ambitious moving beyond the world of religion to encompass economics, politics and culture. There is still much we can learn from the surprisingly radical small power vision that ultimately inspired the American revolution of 1776.

That revolution sparked another insurrectionary period in Europe, in which millions rose up against the authoritarian state and their aristocratic supporters, ushering in a new era of small power in the 19th century although only with limited success. This lasted until the 20th century when the big power vision came to dominate more completely than any other period over the last 500 years.

It was this vision that changed our economy from one centred on a large number of small and medium sized businesses to one dominated by a handful of very large corporations. It was this vision that created governments that control between a third and a half of what is spent in our economies. It was this vision that stifled the free choice of women and anyone who was seen to deviate from the "norm" of heterosexual white male.

This "Big Power Consensus" that shaped the last century exerts such a powerful gravitational pull that we seem unable to operate outside its orbit even now. Governments are still expected to use their power and resources to solve our biggest problems. Now, fewer people and fewer corporations control even more of our economy than was the case 30 years ago. Women and minority groups trying to secure basic freedoms and equality have to constantly struggle against fierce resistance and sometimes violent backlashes.

There is, however, a force defying this gravitational pull, dragging us free of the hierarchy, elitism and inequality of the last century. It is powered by the same fuel that inspired opposition to those same evils back in 1522 when Zwingli sat down for dinner: a deep human desire for freedom.

We can see that desire in the way that populations around the world are growing increasingly frustrated with their closed, hierarchical political elites. It's there in the huge pressures that big business now faces to keep the allegiance of sceptical and often hostile customers. It can be seen in a widespread loss of faith in bureaucratic public services.

A SMALL POWER VISION FOR
THE 21ST CENTURY

If we are to truly escape the gravitational pull of the Big Power Consensus of the last century, that frustration and tension needs, like the American Revolution, to be channelled into support for a much clearer small power vision of the future than is currently on offer from most political parties or movements.

So a large part of this book is given over to understanding what that vision should be. I use the shorthand of the 3 Ds to describe it:

The first D is a wider *distribution* of economic power. The Big Power Consensus concentrated the economy around extremely large corporations. These are entirely owned by their often equally large investors who ultimately control the organisation and, more importantly, enjoy the revenues that flow from the increase in the value of the company's assets and its profits. For the middle decades of the last century the inequality promoted by such concentration of power was mitigated by various factors such as labour shortages and increasing home ownership. But as those conditions have disappeared, concentrated economic power has become the force for inequality it was always bound to be.

The solution outlined here, however, is not to establish a big state to act as a countervailing force to big business and inequality as promoted by socialists in the 20th century and still promoted by many today. That approach not only simply replaces one form of elitist hierarchy with another, but it also fails to take into account the many shifts in technology, demographics and public attitudes which make such a statist strategy impossible.

Instead, the book outlines the beginnings of a programme that uses state power to reform the rules of the economy so that the financial benefits of wealth and ownership flow automatically to as many people as possible, avoiding the need for the government to constantly tax and transfer income.

The second D is a shift towards *direct* democracy and away from representative systems. It also stands for a shift towards *direct* spending of tax revenues by the users of public services rather than by politicians and officials. Both of these represent a sharing out of political power among a nation's citizens rather than its concentration in the hands of a political and bureaucratic elite characteristic of last century's Big Power Consensus. It is also proposed as the only meaningful solution to deepening alienation from democratic political systems across the advanced economies. This is the bitter outcome of the old big institutions' failure to adapt to a world where people increasingly believe they have a right to be heard and to have an influence over what is done in their name.

The final and third D is the vision of truly *diverse* societies where people are free to choose their own lifestyles and where the conformist dreams that prevailed in the middle of the last century are consigned to the rubbish heap. That big cultural consensus was always far weaker than the economic and polit-ical consensus and unsurprisingly more progress has been made over the last 40 years to a small power culture than in the other areas. However, as the history of big versus small power reveals, those who are keen to impose their moralities on others are never far away. Such groups have made political progress in recent years both in the developing and advanced economies. Their potential to disrupt the progress towards diversity should not be underestimated and they must be resisted.

These 3 Ds aim to revive the spirit of radicalism that be-lieved human progress was best served by allowing people to flourish freely and equally outside the grip of large hierarchical organisations and the concentrations of power and wealth that accompany them. It is a spirit that was killed by the big power obsessions of the last century, but it is one, I firmly believe, whose time has come again.

2

The Great Fact

ALL HELL BROKE LOOSE

Imagine yourself taking a trip to stay with your great, great, great, great, great, great, great, great grandparents. You have about 500 pairs so it should not be difficult to discover the ones that match the global average of the time. This will make sure you get the most representative experience of life in the early years of the 18th century.[1]

Once you get used to the strange accents, the unfamiliar words, the alien manners and, let's face it, the tolerance for very human odours, you will have to get on with living. Chances are, given this is an average family, you will spend much of your day working hard in the fields nurturing a staple crop. No matter what the weather, you will be out there bent double in the beating sun, driving rain or scarring wind. After a few hours of that, you will have some animals to feed, water and muck out. In the evening, a member of your family may take pity on you and help you learn a simple task or craft to support the household; maybe washing clothes, open fire cooking, spinning, sewing or basic carpentry. And then the

---

1   Data in this section is from Angus Maddison, *The World Economy: Historical Statistics*

sun goes down; after a few songs and maybe a simple game or two, it is bedtime.

No doubt after some weeks of this sinew stiffening and mind-numbing routine, you will be looking forward to the sabbath like the truest of true believers, even if most of that day is taken up with prayer and silent contemplation.

Your life will not always be so mundane. There will be the odd public holiday when the local villages celebrate with singing, dancing and a fair bit of heavy drinking – assuming the cultural and religious practices observed by your relatives allow for such pleasures. There will be trips to town now and then on bustling market days. But despite these occasional distractions, you are bound to wonder what you get in return for those six demanding days of labour a week.

Most of it will not come in cash, but in food, clothing and shelter. However, for the sake of simplicity, let us convert all of that into dollars at today's prices. This may give you a better idea of your 18th century income. It is hardly a princely sum – around one and a half dollars a day or, to be precise, $616 a year. Think what that might buy you today and you will get a sense of what the average person survived on in the early 1700s. Save it up for two or three days and in today's New York, London or Paris you might be able to afford a decent, cheap meal. Spend it every day and you are looking at a couple of snacks and a soft drink, or maybe a child's meal at a fast-food restaurant. Pretty soon you will probably decide on a daily intake of boiled cereals or pulses. Not tasty but filling and, most of all, cheap. Probably not that dissimilar to what your adoptive 18th century family laid on the table day in, day out.

To be fair, that $616 a year is the global *average* for 1700. If your ancestors were lucky enough to live in one of the most "advanced" economies of the time (Belgium, Denmark, Italy or Britain) they would have enjoyed an income closer to

$1,000. Think what $2 to $3 could buy you today and lick your lips.

Find yourself living in the absolute economic powerhouse of the time – Holland – and you will be touching the dizzy heights of $2,130 a year: double the global average.

If this is all rather difficult to believe, consider that living into your 50s in the 1700s put you among the ranks of the long-lived. Average life expectancy in England, for example, was 35 years. Of course this figure is partly explained by the fact that medical science was worse than useless, public health was a concept yet to be invented and infant mortality was horribly high. But fundamentally, life and work were physically hard, while diet was poor. Giving up the ghost after four or so decades was not a surprising outcome.

So bid your relatives a not so fond farewell and rush back to the 21st century as fast as you can. What will you find when you get back?

You may be struck immediately by the fact that the average yearly global income today is around $6,500 – a 10-fold increase in just eight generations. In the most advanced economies, it is closer to $20,000. That is a 20-fold increase in income. For some countries that were dirt poor in 1700 but are very comfortable now (Finland, Norway and Japan), it is more like a factor of 30.

Imagine shifting from surviving in one of today's richest cities on a daily income of $3 a day to $54 a day. Like winning the lottery surely.

Such a growth in wealth over such a short period of time is remarkable not just for the improvement in human existence it has wrought but also because it reveals a truly amazing historical shift. Average income per head of around $2.50 dollars a day in the early 1700s does not represent some historical low point or grim blip. Quite the opposite. For the 130,000 years since Homo sapiens first emerged on the plains of

Africa, humankind managed to work themselves up to a *peak* of $2.50 dollars a day. If you think 1700 sounds tough, be thankful you were not transported back to 1AD where you would have been struggling along on around $1.20 a day and would have a life expectancy of 25 years.

Humankind managed to grow their incomes by about three times in the space of 130 millennia and then grew it by 10 to 30 times in just two and half centuries. Or as the economist Eric Beinhocker put it: "To summarise . . . economic history in brief: for a very, very, very long time not much happened; then all of a sudden, all hell broke loose."

CANDLES AND TECTONIC SHIFTS

But there is more to this change than simple quantity. Those numbers fail to communicate the revolution that has occurred in the quality of the products and services we now purchase compared to 250 years ago. If we are really trying to understand how much better off we are, we must surely incorporate this element of quality as well.

Indeed, if we were to take the greater material benefit and ease we now enjoy into account, then the figures for income per head are surely exceptionally conservative.

William Nordhaus is an economist who has taken this problem seriously. He uses an example that all in the developed world now take for granted: artificial light. Nordhaus calculated that to achieve 1,000 lumen hours of lighting from a burning fire, our hunter-gatherer relatives would have had to put in around 50 hours of labour, nearly all spent collecting fuel. Neolithic oil lamps were only slightly less costly. The invention of the candle was a real leap – reducing the labour needed to five hours – and the best 19th century gas lamps took a quarter of an hour or more.

These advances, however, dim into insignificance compared to those that have been made since 1900 – particularly through the use of electricity – with our world now being lit up with a fraction of a second's labour. But the real question here is not just how much more light we can buy with our labour but how much brighter, vivid and useable our surroundings are as a result.

We have moved from the dim ambience of a wood fire on a dark night, to the flickering glow of a candle, to the reliable glare of electric light that can compete with the brightest sunlit day. Light is not only much cheaper, it is also much higher quality and our lives are incalculably better as a result. Think of your ancestors with their songs and games before bed not long after the sun went down. For them, darkness really meant something.

Other examples are easy to come by. A well-stocked library is no longer a sign of great wealth but instead simply indicates the fulfilment of a powerful desire to learn. Grandparents can now see real-time moving and speaking images of their growing grandchildren who live many miles away, rather than waiting for the occasional letter or crackly phone call. And any attempt to assess the deepening of human experience brought about by new forms of transport, from the bicycle to the jetliner, could well produce enough words to fill that well-stocked library.

Nordhaus has been more methodical. Taking a long list of different areas of consumption, he reckons they fall into three categories:

1. Those that have undergone "run of the mill" improvements over the last 200 or so years. These include clothing, furniture and personal care.

2. Those that have enjoyed "seismic" change; meaning the goods are still fundamentally recognisable when

compared to the early 19th century, but have seen great improvements in quality. Here he puts categories such as cleaning, watches, housing and education.

3. Finally, there are areas of consumption that have seen "tectonic" change, with products fundamentally transformed compared to 200 years ago. Nordhaus places household appliances, telephones, medical care, transport and electronics here.

He estimates that no less than three-quarters of all the products we surround ourselves with fall into the tectonic category. So the discoveries of the last 250 years have not only radically increased the amount of stuff we can buy, but have also vastly enhanced the quality of that stuff.

It is difficult to quantify this in financial terms (that is part of the point) but the brave Nordhaus has had a stab. He reckons that between 1800 and 1992 – if we take into account the actual improvement in the quality of the things we use – real income per head has increased not by around 10 times but by anything between 40 and 190 times.

12 BILLION THINGS AND COUNTING

Alongside quantity and quality, there is a third aspect to this historical shift: the increase in the diversity of what we are able to purchase.

Eric Beinhocker has attempted to work out the extent of the increase in diversity. Using a calculation based on the bar code system that assigns a unique number to every commodity, he estimates that our economy is currently flooded with about 12 billion different products. He puts that in perspective by pointing out that such a figure vastly outstrips the number of species on earth, which at upper estimates, are numbered at around a measly one billion.

How does this compare to our hunter-gatherer or early farmer selves? Looking at current examples of human societies that still operate under these older economic conditions, Beinhocker reckons somewhere between 300 and 800 items were available for use and exchange.

Although, Beinhocker does not discuss the 1700s in this context, given what we know about the very significant rise in purchasing power since then, it is surely safe to assume that while our 18th century selves probably had a much wider choice than our Stone Age relatives, the bulk of that explosion from around 800 goods to 12 billion goods must have occurred in the last 250 years.

These figures are well-informed guesses but they do give a good sense of the scale of the change we have enjoyed. In fact, they may be quite conservative guesses. Beinhocker has focused on the sorts of tangible products you can slip in a shopping basket. If one were to include the vast range of services now available – everything from plumbers and plasterers, to accountants and aromatherapists – the sheer scope of the marketplace is enough to induce vertigo.

This unprecedented historic shift in the quantity, quality and diversity of the products we use means we live more varied, more entertaining, more comfortable, more fascinating, more thrilling, tastier, sportier, colourful lives than even our grandparents. Think about all the products and services that give you joy. Not just shallow three-minute joy but great days out with friends and families or constant online connection with loved ones – joy. Notice how many of them were not around 50 years ago.

SMALL POWER AND 250 YEARS OF
UNPRECEDENTED PROGRESS

A casual observer might assume that Deirdre McCloskey is a conventional academic. She is a Distinguished Professor of Economics at the University of Illinois at Chicago who has published over 400 scholarly essays and 16 books. She spent over a decade teaching at one of the most prestigious and influential economics departments in the world at the University of Chicago. But take a look at the subtitle of her latest book: *Why Economics Can't Explain the Modern World*. Consider the fact that she has spent a good part of her career politely telling her colleagues that their obsession with mathematical models and statistics doesn't mean they are approaching anything close to scientific truth about the economy; and that she is as happy undertaking detailed studies of history, philosophy and even literature to understand the economy – it becomes clear that Prof. McCloskey is no ordinary economist.

She also has another claim to unconventionality. Until the age of 53 she was Donald McCloskey. In the mid-1990s, she underwent sex reassignment surgery, a process she wrote about in her book *Crossing: A Memoir* . To say this is unusual, not to mention brave in the rather staid world of academic economics, is an understatement.

So Deirdre McCloskey is something of a proud inheritor of the legacy of the small power revolution. She is a freethinker and critic of the very world that has showered her with honours and given her a sparkling career. She has been free to not only assert that she has a different gender to the one she was born with but actually change that gender. She is an unconventional human being living in a world where she has the power to make those unconventional choices rather than being told how to think and behave by someone holding the power elsewhere.

Look at Deirdre McCloskey and you look at a world transformed by small power – a world where millions of people have the freedom and the power to make an uncountable number of little choices for themselves where once they were constrained by the looming presence of a domineering state, a controlling religious hierarchy or an exploitative class of landowners and aristocrats.

This, in itself, might be enough to recommend small power thinking and practice over its alternative but McCloskey's unconventional thinking helps explain a far wider and hugely beneficial economic legacy of small power. McCloskey is fascinated by the huge advances in human wealth and welfare of the last 250 years. She calls that advance the Great Fact and has done more than probably any other person to understand its causes.

The magisterial culmination of this work was her book, *Bourgeois Dignity* – it's the one with the unexpected subtitle. In this book she surveys all the many reasons economists and historians have supplied for the Great Fact. The growth of foreign trade is often given as a cause, but as McCloskey shows, it was still very small when the sudden growth in economies and incomes took off.

Some have argued that the expansion of European empires explains the trend but as she points out, imperial conquest had been a feature of human history for millennia and the expansion happened after the Great Fact began and generally cost European nations more in economic terms than they benefitted.

A popular theory, particularly on the right of the political spectrum, is that the establishment of firmly enforced rights of ownership allowed trade to flourish and wealth to grow. But again, McCloskey points out such rights were firmly established in places such as China that did not enjoy the Great Fact until very recently.

Maybe it could be the scientific revolution that enabled the innovation that lay behind economic growth from the late 17th century. McCloskey reasonably mentions that the Arab world practised a far more sophisticated science long before Europe and even then the scientific revolution largely focused at the time on abstract issues that were of little practical use.

McCloskey shows that the only cause that stands up to scrutiny and was unique to Holland and Britain, where the Great Fact first began, was the granting of both liberty and dignity to economic innovators and entrepreneurs.

It was a shift away from a world that valued the orthodoxy, grandeur and might of monarchy, aristocracy and Church, towards one that valued the small projects of individual traders, the obsessive ideas of thousands of inventors, the minutiae that existed in a humble merchant's book of sale that allowed the Great Fact to happen.

The legal right to trade freely without interference from the big state was vital. The decline of the meddlesome mindset associated with the absolute monarchies of the 17th and 18th centuries was key here. But equally, and less tangibly, it was the dignity given to entrepreneurial behaviours that allowed them to flourish.

For centuries, the trader was seen as an outsider, a profiteer loyal only to making money rather than the big institutions that dominated European nations. But the decline in respect for these institutions, the valuing of individual freedom, the recognition that countries could benefit from the activities of all of its people rather than just an elite, changed this. The low-born entrepreneur, the middle-class innovator, the merchant who bought low and sold high became something to be honoured, encouraged and imitated.

McCloskey quotes a statement of the great economist

Robert Lucas to explain this liberty and dignity for the humble economic opportunist that could stand as a mission statement for the small power vision that drove the Great Fact:

> . . . for income growth to occur in a society, a large fraction of people must experience changes in the possible lives they imagine for themselves and their children . . . In other words . . . economic development requires a million mutinies.

One very important consequence, of which maybe Mc-Closkey does not make enough, is that financial reward could now flow to those commercial innovators and entrepreneurs. For the first time, a serious share of a nation's wealth belonged to those who generated change and improvement – as judged by their many customers – rather than to those who happened to be born to the right family or had enough military power to seize those resources.

Not only did this incentivise and further dignify those entrepreneurs and innovators at the heart of this small economic power revolution, but it meant significant resources could be used for further innovation and trade. Where once any surplus generated by an economy was used to support the indolent life of the aristocratic class, or worse, the murderous wars in which they indulged, now it was being used to develop more efficient and cheaper ways to grow crops, produce clothing, light homes, transport goods and so on and so on.

In short, small power and the Great Fact became inseparable.

A GREATER FACT AWAITS

Considering the gap between your life and that of your mid-18th century family may be mind-boggling. Consider the gap between your life and that of your mid-23rd century family and we move from mind-boggling to mind-blowing.

If small power continues to do its work rewarding and dignifying those who innovate and improve, those who think and act differently, those who challenge established institutions and orthodoxy then your great, great, great, great, great, great, great, great grandkids could be 10 times richer than you (even if they're not particularly wealthy for their time) and be living a life of far greater choice, opportunity, experience and joy.

In fact, there is a very strong possibility that the advances of the next 250 years will massively outstrip what came before. The enterprise and innovation that Deirdre McCloskey identified as so crucial to the Great Fact was always a largely elite affair reserved for a select group of engineers, technicians and business people. As later chapters will show, those entrepreneurial behaviours are now increasingly widespread, driven by small power values that inspire billions rather than thousands to seek self-expression, creative change and challenge to established interests.

Under these conditions of mass enterprise and innovation, the opportunity for increasingly rapid improvement in the quantity, quality and diversity of products is that much greater. The economic vibrancy, benefits and growth of the next two and a half centuries could be historically unparalleled. However, there is no guarantee that small power will continue unimpeded. The popular appetite may be there, but the big power institutions and values of the last century cling on and in some ways have strengthened their hold. The Great Fact is at risk of dissolving into a Great Contradiction where the mass desire for creativity and enterprise is constantly stifled by those determined to hold on to their positions of power, wealth and influence.

This book is dedicated to understanding how and why this Great Contradiction is emerging. More importantly it seeks to explain how it can be resolved.

Section II

SMALL POLITICS: TOWARDS DIRECT AND DELIBERATIVE DEMOCRACY

3

Big Government Begins

The hierarchical Church obsessed with orthodoxy against which Zwingli and Luther rebelled had not always been a bastion of big power. For a millennium, Christianity had been based on a wide variety of local practices and beliefs. But from the 11th century onwards, a succession of popes imposed an increasingly centralised control and uniformity. Protests against this assertion of power were destroyed and then used as an excuse to enforce even greater control. A classic case was the 14th century revolt against Church hierarchy led by John Wycliffe, which led not only to the crushing of Wycliffe and his followers, but the banning of all translations of the Bible not authorised by the Church. However, the new wave of "heresy" led by Zwingli and Luther, with its contrasting of individual freedom of choice against the authority of the religious hierarchy, caught the imagination of Northern Europe like never before.

Over the next few years, what the historian Franz Lau called a "wildwuchs," or wild fire of the sort that sweeps through parched forests, took hold. Printing, that new exciting information technology, exploded in the wake of Luther and Zwingli's revolution with millions of copies of sermons, writings and pamphlets by the Reformation's leaders being published and distributed across Europe. Many thousands of priests, monks and nuns eagerly denounced their vows of celibacy, found partners and married. Villages and towns across the northern part of the continent declared their religious independence from the Catholic Church. Most notably, millions of ordinary people stopped paying the taxes the Church demanded of them. And as is often the case with revolutions, a wing emerged that rapidly outstripped and shocked the movement's founders with its radicalism. The so-called Anabaptists completely rejected the authority not just of the Catholic Church but of any religious hierarchy.

The Anabaptists baptised each other and distributed the bread and wine of the traditional Christian Church service among themselves. In their view, true faith had no need of priests at all. Some extended their radicalism beyond the bounds of religion by calling on all Christians to refuse to serve in the army or swear oaths of allegiance to any Lord other than Christ. Most scandalously, some Anabaptist congregations were led by women, at a time, of course, when the inferiority of women was almost entirely unquestioned.

For the original leaders of the rebellion, this more radical version of small power went too far. The flame of radicalism in Zwingli's own city of Zurich was rapidly doused when four Anabaptist leaders were executed by drowning only a few months after their festival of self-baptism. Anabaptists in Moravia who followed the example of some early Christian communities by denying their personal property and living communally, became refugees when their leaders were executed. Even Strasbourg, probably the most tolerant city in Europe, and a haven for many varieties of Protestantism, executed an Anabaptist called Thomas Saltzmann who questioned the divinity of Christ.

This conservative turn was deepened by a new generation of Protestant reformers led by John Calvin, a French priest based in Geneva. During the 1540s and 1550s, Calvin destroyed the more fringe elements of the Reformation – most famously by demanding the execution of the radical Michael Servetus. But more importantly, he established clear institutional structures for Protestantism that were just as attached to orthodoxy and hierarchy as the Catholic Church.

Over the next 50 years, Protestantism came to dominate nearly half of the land mass of Europe, including much of Eastern and Central Europe and even some of northern Italy. But war, violent oppression, and missionary work by a renewed Catholicism shocked into its own reform, meant Protestantism was ultimately pushed back into Northern Germany, Switzerland, the Netherlands and England by the end of the 17th century. The Catholic Church had regained a great deal of what it had lost in territorial terms but it was never to play as significant a part in public life as it once had. In its place, a new force, the nation state, emerged as the flag bearer for centralised, hierarchical authority.

WAR GIVES BIRTH TO THE STATE

National governments as we understand them today did not exist before the 17th century. The vast majority of people lived extremely local lives. Transport was slow, uncomfortable and expensive, but more importantly, the world was structured around oaths in which each member of a class would swear obedience and loyalty to the next tier up. As a result, the great mass of people owed their allegiance to their local aristocratic landowner rather than any larger regional, let alone national power.

States were tiny and largely concerned with fighting battles based on hastily cobbled together armies, which disbanded as soon as the fighting ceased. Even the capacity of the monarchs who fought those wars relied very heavily on persuading their nobles to agree to temporary taxes to fund the wars and to allow their peasants to join the fight.

But this haphazard and fragmented approach to running things could no longer guarantee victory during the long period of military conflict in the 1600s sparked by the Reformation. Gradually it became clear that armies and the governments that led them would have to become far better organised, more permanent and centralised than they previously were.

Nowhere was this logic taken to greater extremes than in France, which was to be the pre-eminent force in Europe during the troubled 17th century. France had been particularly hard hit by the Reformation. Calvin's message leaked across the Swiss border ultimately inspiring a home-grown French Protestantism in the form of the Huguenot movement. By the early 1560s, religious differences merged with tensions between regions and classes as economic problems caused hardship across the country.

The tension exploded into violent conflict when the most powerful nobleman in the country, the Duke of Guise, had his soldiers burn down a church, killing dozens of the Huguenots barricaded inside in the town of Vassy. This brutal event kicked off 35 years of bloodletting and misery that killed over two million people and was punctuated by horrendous atrocities on both sides, including the notorious St. Bartholomew's Day Massacre, which saw approximately 10,000 Huguenots slaughtered by mobs in one terrible week across France.

The economic devastation wrought by the conflict inspired furious revolts by peasants towards the end of the century. The nobility who had been killing each other for over three decades began to put their differences aside and unite in the face of this threat from below. The result was that by the 1590s, a new French state began to emerge under the leadership of King

Henry IV of the noble Bourbon family. This state not only had a united aristocracy behind it but had the wartime spirit and techniques of command and control embedded in its very soul.

THE SUN KING RISES

For the first time, Paris was established as the home of the monarchy and was rebuilt in grand style to symbolise the move. Catholicism was adopted as the official religion of the nation. No national parliament was called, sidelining many lower classes of nobility from any decision-making process. When Henry's son Louis XIII succeeded to the throne in 1610, the pace of change only speeded up.

The King's chief minister, Cardinal Richelieu, immortalised in Alexander Dumas's classic novel as the ruthless enemy of the three musketeers, set about crushing any remnants of Huguenot resistance and destroyed any nobles who refused to accept the new order. Most importantly, he established a new cadre of officials appointed directly by the King to administer law and order and finance across the towns and cities of France undermining the traditional powers of local aristocrats.

This increasingly efficient and powerful centralised state became ever better at collecting taxes. Between 1610 and 1644, income from the *taille*, the main tax, grew from 17 million livres (the French currency of the day) to 44 million livres.[2]

This new tax burden sparked revolts across the country. But the efficient structures established by Richelieu were strong and the five-year rebellion was brutally suppressed. This victory left the new breed of state even more powerful, just in time for the coronation of the ultimate absolutist monarch, Louis XIV, in 1654.

---

2   Perry Anderson, *Lineages of the Absolutist State*

Under the so-called Sun King, the centralisation and expansion of state power was taken to ever-greater heights. The country was split into 32 regions in which the officials, established by Richelieu, now ruled with enormous and unchallengeable powers. The senior nobility was literally centralised being required to live in the Versailles Palace near Paris under the watchful eye of the King himself. A permanent police force was established across the whole country and the army grew during Louis's reign by 10 times from around 30,000 to 300,000.[3] Most importantly, this was a new type of army: well-drilled, well-paid, uniformed and permanent, owing its allegiance to the King and no one else. The rag-tag conglomerations of sullen peasants that had fought wars in previous centuries were a distant memory.

None of this was cheap of course, and tax revenues continued to rise, doubling in just a decade. Revolts began again but they were, as before, ferociously crushed. Louis used the same force to reimpose religious orthodoxy on the country by expelling all remaining Huguenots a few years later.

Money was also raised by turning the state into a business. The King established, controlled and held major financial interests in trades as wide as cloth, ironware and glass. Punitive tariffs were put in place to ensure that no overseas merchant or foreign state could undermine the monarchy's investments and revenue streams.

None of this was accidental. There was a clear rationale developed to explain why this "absolutism" was necessary and good. Political, economic and religious justifications were developed and widely debated in France and across Europe.

In political terms, the all-powerful monarch was lauded as the guarantor of security and even freedom. Thomas Hobbes, the enormously influential English philosopher, was the most

---

3   Perry Anderson, *Lineages of the Absolutist State*

sophisticated proponent of such views in the 17th century. He argued that while humans are entirely free to do as they want under the laws of nature, such freedom is ultimately self-defeating. A world where everyone seizes that freedom would ultimately degenerate into violent conflict in which the strongest and most aggressive succeeded at the expense of the weaker. The only solution to this fundamental problem was to invest power in a powerful ruler who could lay down and enforce rules for civilised behavior, ensuring that at least some semblance of freedom was able to exist. It was an argument that seemed to make sense in a period which had been scarred by decades of war and violent atrocities. Life had, for many decades, seemed "nasty, brutish and short", to use Hobbes's well-worn phrase, for many of the peoples of France and Northern Europe for decades.

The argument was not only timely; it was also forward-looking and radical. In our democratic era, we tend to think of authoritarian ideals as old-fashioned and reactionary. But Hobbes was regarded as a dangerous radical. His notion that freedom meant essentially doing what you wanted could not have contrasted more strongly with traditional ideas which saw freedom as essentially a religious ideal which meant escaping from the bonds of human desire into the arms of God and the Church. In essence, Hobbes had taken the spirit of individual freedom of choice, first launched by the Reformation, and turned it brilliantly on its head to argue for just the sort of hierarchy and orthodoxy against which the early Protestants had been rebelling.

Tellingly, when Hobbes left England in a hurry, fearing arrest by the anti-monarchical forces of Oliver Cromwell, it was to Paris he fled. He was welcomed with open arms by the city's intellectuals.

Absolutism's modern feel did not stop at the political. New ideas placed a strong state at the heart of economic progress.

The dominant view was that precious metals were the source of a nation's wealth. This was, after all, the era of colonial expansion in the Americas, which was generating a vibrant trade in gold and silver. The new wealth created a merchant class with the money to spend on finer clothes, elaborate homes and artwork. There was, however, only so much precious metal available and hence wealth was regarded as a zero-sum game. The more wealth one nation had, the less another could enjoy. It made sense to such an analysis to give a monarch the power to protect a country's wealth and, particularly, its stock of precious metal by keeping out foreign business competition and, when necessary, using military might to seize money and trade from other countries.

It would be over a century after the accession of Louis XIV before the economist Adam Smith would strike a fatal blow against this "mercantilist" mindset, arguing convincingly – and as it was to prove, correctly – that wealth was not fixed but could keep on growing to the benefit of all nations engaged in peaceful trading.

Louis and his imitators across Europe also seized on a new religious justification for centralised monarchical power: the divine right of kings. First developed by the philosopher Jean Bodin in the midst of France's bloody religious wars and then taken up by James I of England, the idea was relatively simple but inspired a great deal of scholarly work and debate. It was argued by Bodin and James that monarchs are an expression of God's will by virtue of the very fact that they have been born into that position. An omnipotent God could clearly choose to put anyone on the throne but he chose that particular person.

This means that a monarch is accountable to no one but his or her maker. Again this may sound to our ears like a strikingly old-fashioned position but this, of course, contrasted with centuries of history where monarchs had constantly struggled to secure the support of their nobles and parliaments to wage war and raise taxes. This new arrangement could claim to be progress compared to the chaos of the past.

Importantly, this was not seen as a justification for tyranny. Bodin and others were clear that a king was *genuinely* accountable to God, which meant behaving in a moral and just fashion. In the final instance, however, such good behaviour was a matter for the monarch's conscience and God's judgement, not that of any earthly power such as a parliament. Again, it was an idea that felt very much of its time, stressing the direct relationship between the monarch and the creator at a time when Protestantism had placed the individual's close link to God at the heart of their religious vision.

For the middle decades of the 17th century, France was regarded widely as the most advanced and powerful state in Europe. The model of absolutist monarchy put in place by three kings of the Bourbon family with its powerful bureaucracy, large modern army, efficient taxation and tight economic control was imitated across the continent having particular influence in Spain, Portugal, Prussia in modern Germany and Piedmont in modern Italy. The combination of endless war, French administrative genius and Bourbon ruthlessness established the modern state as we still know it today with its standing professional army, permanent taxes and sophisticated bureaucracy.

Big government had been born.

4

Radical America

Gottlieb Mittelberger was a German schoolteacher who left his home in May 1750 to travel to Pennsylvania in America. His plan was to join the growing, vibrant colony there established by his countrymen. He would have known that the journey across the Atlantic was likely to be uncomfortable. Long distance travel in the 18th century, even on land, was not something to be decided upon lightly, but nothing prepared him for the horrors of the two months he spent at sea.

As Mittelberger wrote mournfully in his account of the journey, the ship was a scene of "terrible misery: stench, fumes, horror, vomiting, many kinds of sea-sickness, fever, dysentery, headache, heat, constipation, boils, scurvy, cancer, mouth rot, and the like, all of which come from old and sharply salted food and meat, also from very bad and foul water, so that many die miserably."

Lice were so endemic that the parasites could be scraped off the body in clumps. Thirty-two children died on Mittelberger's ship, mostly from measles or smallpox. In a severe storm a woman died in labour because no help could be given to her in such perilous conditions. Her body was pushed unceremoniously through a porthole into the sea below. Indeed, Mittelberger recounts that despite the intense suffering, nothing was worse than the storms, which could last for days leaving the passengers in a state of constant terror.

Why so many were willing to risk Mittelberger's grim experience is an indication of how for many Europeans, America was becoming a land of hope and freedom when Europe was stuck in a period of despair and oppression. A large number went to escape the deep and widespread rural poverty of their homeland; to leave behind societies where the chances of breaking out of your preordained class were extremely small given the great power still wielded by noble families and the Church. If you could afford to pay your passage to America, you would be rewarded with 50 acres of land under the "headright" system and you could be established as an independent farmer – a truly remarkable thing given that much of Europe still laboured under a feudal system in which peasants worked land owned by an aristocrat.

Many others were motivated by religion. Depressed by the failure of the Reformation to deliver continent-wide change, America seemed to offer an opportunity to set up new societies free of persecution and built on sounder biblical principles than those operating across Europe. This was the motivation for the small group of early settlers known as the Pilgrim Fathers. They belonged to a radical Protestant congregation that suffered imprisonment and harassment in England for their refusal to attend Church of England services. They set up their colony in Plymouth, Massachusetts in 1620; a settlement regarded by Americans as one of the main founding events for their nation. The annual US celebration of Thanksgiving can be traced back to a similar celebration in Plymouth.

This meant that while large parts of the European continent were subject to a generation of monarchs keen to emulate the big power of Louis XIV, a completely different society was being constructed in the exotic, backwater world of the American colonies.

When Gottlieb Mittelberger finally made it to Philadelphia he was amazed by this different society. He was stunned by how cheap goods were and by the fact that there was no need for a city wall to keep out invaders: in fact, he noted the constant inward and outward flow of merchants.

He was astounded by the freedom and diversity. People of many different religions mixed happily with each other. Ordinary people were free to preach on matters of faith without fear of persecution. He recounts with bemusement a Quaker service where the members of the congregation discussed the rights and wrongs of the sermon at great length.

This spirit of freedom meant early Americans were suspicious of, resentful of and resistant to any attempt to impose centralised hierarchy to control or weaken this diversity. There was a general dislike of government or of economic domination. Mittelberger was very struck, for example, by the way anyone in America could simply set themselves up in any trade without the fear that they would be threatening the monarchy's business interests or the rules imposed by some small elite of local businessmen.

Even those settlers who imported John Calvin's hierarchical and authoritarian structures found it difficult to maintain their theocracy in the face of the colonial spirit of rebellion and freedom. Remarkable figures like Anne Hutchinson, a Boston midwife, led regular attempts to overturn the strict orthodox rule of the Puritans, which could often stretch beyond the Church and into government.

King Charles II of England, however, had little enthusiasm for America's small power spirit. When he was restored to the throne in 1660 after the 11-year rule of Oliver Cromwell, which followed the execution of Charles's father, he became determined to crush this "New England Disease". He appointed Edmund Andros as effective dictator of the region. Andros rapidly set about transplanting the absolutist ways of Europe:

raising taxes to fund military expansion, banning any printed expression of dissent, controlling commercial activity and declaring the established system of land ownership rights – based on the headright principle – void.

This attempt to turn small power America into big power Europe failed miserably. Rebellions spread rapidly across the colonies against the agents of the monarchy in what looks now like a dress rehearsal for the struggle almost a century later to finally throw off British rule altogether. Andros himself was imprisoned for 10 months before being allowed to return to England. The story of his attempt to escape his captors, disguised in a dress and lady's wig – which was widely shared at the time to the great amusement of the American colonists – is, sadly, probably untrue.

SMALL POWER REBELS

It was into this culture of freedom, rebellion and independence that a short, pale, shy man with a tendency to hypochondria was born. He was an unlikely revolutionary leader, given his personality, but James Madison Jr. was destined to play a fundamental role in embedding the small power principles he grew up with at the heart of the new independent nation of the United States of America. In doing so, however, he was first to become a close ally and friend, and then a sworn enemy, of another guiding figure of the new American nation, Alexander Hamilton – a man with a very different, bigger power vision for the future of his country.

James Madison was the much-loved first son of one of the wealthiest families in mid-18th century Virginia. His father was a plantation owner relying on the work of over 100 slaves to generate his fortune. As the eldest son, James was to inherit the plantation as well as its slaves: a contradiction given his

strong commitment to individual liberty that he never satisfactorily resolved.

Despite his apparently sickly body, his mind proved to be
exceptionally sharp. As a very young man, he was already publishing radical pamphlets which associated him closely with
the growing numbers agitating against British control of the
American colonies.

That agitation soon turned into outright conflict between
militias of American rebels and British troops trying to enforce
order. A year after this revolutionary war started, the rebels
took the momentous step of declaring the 13 colonies independent of British rule. The violence inevitably escalated.
Madison was elected to the Virginia state legislature in this
highly charged period at the age of just 25. He immediately
became deeply involved in the writing of Virginia's Declaration
of Rights.

Madison quickly made a name for himself opposing an
attempt to introduce a clause into Virginia's declaration
requiring toleration of other faiths in the colony. His objection
was that the proposal did not go far enough. Madison did not
want just toleration for faiths, he wanted it made clear that
Virginia's citizens had the right to expect full and equal
freedom to be able to practise and choose whatever religion
they desired. He also unsuccessfully tried to secure the abolition of slavery in the colony. The historical line from the early
Reformation through to the ideals that inspired the man now
known as the father of the US Constitution is clear.

Ultimately, however, Madison's greatest moment would
come when he was selected as one of Virginia's delegates to the
Philadelphia Convention of 1787 which was tasked, very controversially, with establishing a workable system of government
for the United States of America. The Convention would produce the Constitution, which is still in operation today.

In the wake of the Convention, Madison would form an

unstoppable alliance with Alexander Hamilton, arguing force-fully for a Constitution that provided for a powerful, united but limited government of the USA, which while inevitably reducing the power of state governments would guarantee the freedom of individuals.

If anything, Hamilton was even more precocious than Madison but his route to greatness could not have been more different. He was born into poverty and out of wedlock on the Caribbean island of Nevis. After his father abandoned his mother, the family moved to St. Croix in the Virgin Islands, which was a centre of the booming slave trade. The youthful Alexander's experience of slave auctions and transports made him a lifelong opponent of slavery: unlike Madison he never owned another human being.

Despite the shock of his mother's death when he was only 13, which thrust him into even deeper poverty, the young Alexander managed to gain employment as a clerk at a local trading firm. Here, his powerful intelligence and forceful per-sonality began to show itself. He was soon managing the whole company. What older employees felt at being ordered about by a teenager can be guessed at but throughout his life Hamilton was rarely influenced or knocked off his stride by the views of others.

However, it was an essay he wrote about a hurricane that hit the island that changed the course of his life. Eminent mem-bers of the local business community were impressed and raised the money to send the 17-year-old to school in New Jersey.

Like Madison, Hamilton was an instinctive small power rebel and was soon writing pamphlets denouncing British con-trol of the colonies. In an action, however, that was emblematic of a courageous and lifelong commitment to upholding the law, he pacified a revolutionary mob that was intent on attack-ing the pro-British president of Hamilton's college. Some years later as a successful lawyer in New York, Hamilton would take a similar stand by defending those who had spoken out against the Revolution from prosecution.

Within just three years of arriving in America, Hamilton was fighting for his adoptive country's freedom, captaining an artillery company, which he had personally established in New York. He was soon noticed by the Commander-in-Chief himself, George Washington. Somewhat to Hamilton's disappointment, as it took him away from the battlefield, Washington invited him to be his chief aide – a role he fulfilled with typical competence for four years.

Washington hugely admired the young officer but it was a sentiment not entirely reciprocated. Hamilton felt Washington was often inflexible and unimaginative. Tensions between the men grew. After a bizarre altercation where the two rowed in public about the younger man being a few minutes late for a meeting, Hamilton asked to be found a position back on the battlefield.

Following the war, Hamilton and Madison were elected to Congress – the young nation's parliament – as representatives for New York and Virginia respectively. Both became intensely frustrated by the weakness of the body. Soldiers were close to mutiny demanding back pay and supplies, and America's creditors, of which there were many following the huge cost of the war, were clamouring for the country's debts to be honoured. Congress, however, had no power to raise taxes under its Articles of Confederation unless every state agreed; something they signally refused to do. Rhode Island won a particularly notorious reputation for wielding an effective veto no matter how every other state voted, earning itself the soubriquet "Rogue Island". Disillusioned, Hamilton resigned from Congress and launched a law firm in New York.

In the meantime, Madison and others campaigned to have an elected body established to agree a new system of government. The Philadelphia Convention finally gained approval and both Madison and Hamilton were elected to join the body.

Over the sweltering summer of 1787, which must have been a particular hell for James Madison, who feared that the hot weather made him more prone to illness, the Convention gradually and painstakingly hammered out the US Constitution. Madison was the most assiduous and focused of the delegates. He suggested a middle way between a proposal from New Jersey, which essentially argued for no change on the current arrangement and a proposal from Hamilton himself, which largely removed all power from the states and gave it to a central government. Hamilton's idea, set out in a six-hour speech to the Convention, was so unpopular it never even got debated. Madison's idea, by contrast, secured the majority and was accepted.

The framing of the Constitution was a remarkable step forward in the battle against big power. Here was a document that laid out the rules for a government that was to draw its legitimacy from the assent of the people through the election of a parliamentary chamber. There is no mention of the sort of personal or hereditary leadership that was not only overwhelmingly the norm in Europe at the time, but was still widely regarded as the most advanced form of government. In fact, the power of the US president only gets dealt with in the second section of the document once Congress has been fully described.

This was the complete and total antithesis of the type of absolute power Louis XIV had created for himself by marginalising parliamentary traditions, destroying all opposition to his decrees and proclaiming himself the choice of God. The US Constitution was the concrete result of two and a half centuries in which the free-choice spirit of the Reformation had been transferred from the world of religion to the world of government. From that point on, the days of the absolute monarchs were numbered even if they did not realise it at the time.

However, the real battle for the Constitution was yet to commence. To be adopted, the Constitution had to be endorsed by nine of the 13 states. It was clear, though, that the Constitution would be dead if it did not also secure the support of the two most powerful and populous states: Madison's Virginia and Hamilton's New York. This is when the unlikely alliance of the patrician hypochondriac and the low-born soldier came into its own.

The opponents of change had immediately launched a vociferous, emotional and often personal campaign claiming the framers of the Constitution were betraying the principles of the revolution and would establish a new monarchy no better than the old oppressor, Britain. Hamilton and Madison agreed to write a series of papers that would deliberately take a completely different tone: they would make the case for the Constitution in a highly reasoned way. They would also provide much more detail on how any new government could and should operate.

Their work stretched to the production of no less than 85 papers in under a year. Widely read, particularly by those who had to make the argument for ratification of the Constitution in their state legislatures, Hamilton and Madison's *Federalist Papers* were not just successful interventions in a popular debate of truly historic significance, they became founding documents of the new nation; an authoritative commentary on the Constitution itself. Particular credit must go to Hamilton, who despite being rejected and dismissed at the Philadelphia Convention, had the humility to throw his vast intellectual capacity behind an effort to ensure Madison's baby had a chance to survive beyond infancy.

It is easy in the context of the battle between small and big power to sympathise with those who feared that decentralised state power was being undermined in order to allow big, centralised government to flourish. But that is too simplistic.

Madison and Hamilton were highly conscious of how unique America was at the time. They knew that the tyrants and elites across Europe would be delighted if the American experiment failed. And in the period after victory over the British, it looked very much like it would. Bankruptcy stalked the government, the economy was struggling, the 13 states seemed unable to co-operate with each other even though the hostile forces of Britain, Spain and France were still present on the American continent. In addition, some of the states' governments seemed to be drifting away from the very republican principles of the revolution with European-style corruption and autocracy on the rise.

The solution was clearly better co-ordination from the centre, but it was also the codification and proud declaration of the very principles that had inspired the revolution, so that they could never be undermined. As Madison and Hamilton argued, the Constitution was not about placing central power over the states' powers, it was about creating a clear contract between every American citizen and their government that guaranteed their freedom and rights and clearly limited the power of the state. State legislatures may be constrained by the move, but the freedom of the individual would be guaranteed in perpetuity.

The ratification of the US Constitution and the stabilisation and then flourishing of American society and economy in the next few decades was an enormously significant event in the battle for small power. The fact that the US experiment succeeded was a huge inspiration to the emerging movement for liberal rights, democracy and anti-imperialism that swept across Europe in the 1800s. Revolutionaries and reformers in all European countries looked to America as a model for a different way of organising government and society. It disproved the claims of kings and clerics that only their absolute rule stood between humanity and the chaos that Hobbes had predicted. In short, individual freedom and distributed power *could* sit side by side with order and wealth.

Soon after the ratification, the new government was formed in line with the Constitution. George Washington was easily elected as the first President and Madison was sent by the voters of Virginia to the new Congress. The biggest reward, however, was reserved for Hamilton. Having patched up their differences, Washington appointed the lawyer and military hero as Secretary to the Treasury.

The forthright and charismatic Hamilton rapidly transformed the role into something far more like a Prime Minister, developing plans and policies well beyond the realm of the public finances. A role in which Washington, who seemed to have unlimited admiration for the young man, was happy to acquiesce. Hamilton was soon being compared by the new Congress to Robert Walpole, the politician who ran the British government with an iron fist for two decades in the first half of the 18th century. The comparison was not intended as a compliment. Congressional worries, however, turned into deep fears when it became clear what sort of America Hamilton hoped to create.

Despite his undoubted revolutionary fervour, Hamilton was a strong admirer of Britain. In particular, he envied the way the nation was beginning to make the move from an agricultural to a manufacturing based economy. He also understood well how important the increasingly sophisticated financial markets were to this shift, providing investment for businesses looking to innovate and grow in a far more dynamic and speculative fashion than the farms that were the economic backbone of traditional economies. In turn, he also saw how central the British government was to backing the activities of those financial markets. As a firm patriot, Hamilton believed that America could only become a strong nation if it were to follow Britain's example and reinvent itself as an economy built on finance and manufacturing.

This vision filled much of Congress and a great portion of America's new citizens with horror. For this fearful group, the American Revolution was fought not just to protect republican principles and political freedom but also in pursuit of a much wider vision of society and the economy.

The revolutionaries were certainly disgusted by the vast concentrations of political power that had occurred in Europe but they were also sickened by the way aristocrats and monarchies had seized economic power for themselves. The fact that a small elite controlled wealth was regarded as just as destructive of human freedom as the stifling control of state sanctioned religion and the political tyranny of kings.

Although the revolutionaries were deeply influenced by the thought of John Locke, the great philosopher who proposed the idea that government was a contract between the state and the people to serve the interests of the people, they were also guided by the ideas of James Harrington, a thinker who is largely forgotten today. Harrington, who was driven insane by his imprisonment by Charles II, was one of the first thinkers to understand that the nature of a government was deeply shaped by the nature of the economy. The more concentrated wealth was, the more concentrated political power would be, he argued.

Harrington believed that the monarchy had been overthrown in England because a new, confident wealthy class had emerged when the Tudor kings and queens had sold off large portions of land, once owned by the Church and the Crown, to raise money. However, because wealth had not been distributed much wider, England could not advance beyond a constitutional monarchy. It was a political arrangement that perfectly suited the interests of the new wealthy class created by the Tudors because it guaranteed their freedom and rights while ignoring those of the lower classes.

For Harrington, a genuine republic, which did away with monarchy and valued the freedom of all, could only emerge when wealth was shared out as widely as possible. For this reason, Harrington campaigned as an MP for the abolition of primogeniture, the law that stated that ownership of land could not be broken up but had to be passed on from father to eldest son. He also, more controversially, demanded that it should become illegal to own land worth more than £2,000.

The American revolutionaries took Harrington's view to heart. Their vision was of a republic based on an economy where no one could secure too much economic or political power because land was shared out as equally as possible. In their eyes, the emergence of manufacturing in Britain was not a sign of progress and strength but one of decay and weakness. The new factories that were springing up across the old enemy's landscape were the product of a nation running out of land to farm to support their growing population and to feed the wealthy classes' greed. Britain was desperately turning to the manufacture of pointless luxuries to survive economically. The product, as anyone who visited the factories could see for themselves, was not a brave world of science and enterprise united but a horrendous inequality where a new urban aristocracy grew fat and a new urban poor were worked to death.

America, by contrast, was set on a republican and agrarian course. The land was vast beyond imagining, so as the population grew there was no need to turn to the manufacture of luxuries to keep generating wealth. Instead, the young nation could simply expand west to provide new generations of farmers with their portion of land to work for themselves. So when Alexander Hamilton outlined a vision of America built on manufacturing and started to take steps to turn this into a reality, many were deeply opposed. The Secretary to the Treasury proposed that the government borrow large sums of money to pay off its war debts. The IOUs or bonds could then be traded kick-starting new financial markets. He wanted to set up a national bank run by private interests to invest in new manufacturing enterprises. He proposed the introduction of taxes on imports to prevent competition from foreign manufacturers and to give the government a fund from which it could subsidise domestic business. Hamilton even suggested raising taxes as a way to encourage more entrepreneurial activity by those who would have to increase their incomes to make up for their tax losses.

To Hamilton's dismay the opposition to all of these measures in Congress was led by none other than James Madison. Being a man who never fought shy of a good falling out, Hamilton could not forgive Madison for trying to stymie his plans. Of course, they had had their differences at the Philadelphia Convention but Hamilton could not understand how an intelligent revolutionary like Madison would align himself with naïve egalitarians such as Thomas Jefferson – Washington's Secretary of State and a man doing his best to have Hamilton ejected from the government.

But Madison felt that Hamilton was going much too far. The Constitution and its establishment of a central government was enacted to protect the rights of the individual against the power of the state and to prevent the collapse of the American experiment. Hamilton was proposing a government that would control the economy while conspiring with a new aristocracy of manufacturers to increase their wealth at the expense of the people. This would not only enslave and stupefy the masses but also make the state, a plaything of the wealthy. In short, big power would rule in America just as it did in Europe.

With the support of wealthy financiers and the backing of the deeply respected President, Hamilton managed to secure

Congressional backing for his proposals but only in the face of the seething opposition led by Madison.

The Congressional divide soon hardened into permanent factions with Madison and Jefferson leading the Republican Party on one side and Hamilton, Washington and John Adams, the Vice President, establishing the Federalist Party on the other. The political battle between these two was exceptionally bitter with much of the fight stimulating the rise of partisan newspapers, which immediately took the Constitution's guarantee of free speech at its word and spared no insult or slander.

In purely practical terms, Hamilton proved far more realistic than Madison. He understood better than the Republicans, the direction in which the world was travelling. If America was to be more than an agricultural backwater, it would have to embrace the financial sophistication and new world of manufacturing that was beginning to emerge in Europe. He could also see that Madison and his comrades' rejection of the supposedly decadent luxuries produced by manufacturing firms was little more than high-minded nonsense. Like Adam Smith, whose classic work, *The Wealth of Nations*, was published in the same year America declared its independence, Hamilton recognised the enormous enhancement of well-being and living standards that could flow from the expansion of the international manufacturing trade.

However, while Madison's vision of an egalitarian agrarian idyll may seem hopelessly naïve today, his fears about the long-term impacts of Hamilton's plan proved incisive. In particular, he was deeply concerned that the shift to a manufacturing economy would create a new super-wealthy elite which would seize control of the political system, marginalise and anger the impoverished masses and ultimately create an economy that served their own interests rather than the good of all. In short, he feared that the small power vision of a limited state focused on the public good, guaranteed by a relatively equal distribution of wealth, would disappear to be replaced by concentrated wealth and political power.

Looking back over the social divisions and dehumanisation generated by the rise of industrial economies, and the way politics was regularly corrupted by money over the last two centuries, it is hard to deny that Madison was just as far-sighted as Hamilton if in a very different way. Indeed, even now, surveying the social, political and economic wreckage generated by the banking crash of 2008, it is clear that Madison's challenges to Hamilton about the damage his big economic and political vision might generate, have yet to be satisfactorily answered.

It is one of the aims of this book to try and reconcile Hamilton's vision of a highly entrepreneurial and innovative economy with Madison's hopes for equality and freedom for all, no matter what their background.

5

Europe Ablaze

While Europe had continued to labour under the tyranny of absolutist monarchs, who were convinced that they were appointed by God, America reinvigorated the small power spirit that had begun in the Reformation.

When that spirit finally burst into open revolt against the British Empire, many Europeans were also seized by the small power vision. Here, at last, was a successful example of rebels fighting for equality and freedom casting off the burden of tyranny. A loose movement developed across the continent known as Radicalism. They had no unified programme and no formal organisational structure but they shared the American vision of a world of economic and political equality. They knew very firmly what they were against: monarchy, religious hierarchy, imperial power. Like the Americans, most favoured democracy, national liberation, fairer economic shares and free thought and reason.

Maybe quicker than most expected, they had their own example of a successful revolution when in 1789 French Radicals rose up (backed by a very disgruntled peasantry), executed the Bourbon king, Louis XVI, and swept away the aristocracy in the name of equality, liberty and fraternity. This momentous event in the very nation that had refined absolutism to its purest grade sent tremors through the continent.

In Britain, as in other European nations, Radicals who had once seemed like cranks operating on the fringes of society took on a more menacing appearance in the eyes of the political establishment. The widely revered essayist and member of parliament, Edmund Burke, gave voice to establishment fears, publishing a pamphlet attacking the French Revolution and its ideals.

His widely read work was a plea for respect for the status quo that existed in Britain of a limited monarchy governing with a parliament chosen by a small electorate of the propertied classes. Burke rejected the notion of universal rights that had inspired the American and French rebels, dismissed the idea of democracy and made a scathing attack on one of the leaders of the English Radicals, Richard Price.

The first to reply was an unknown Radical called Mary Wollstonecraft who had found her quick temper and fierce intelligence sparked by the reactionary pamphlet. Mary had good reason to be enraged by the complacent conservatism that ran throughout Burke's writings. At the age of 30 she had already exhausted the few options open to an independent-minded woman who did not want to face a lifetime as the property of her husband. She had been a schoolmistress, a governess and even a "companion" to a wealthy female patron for the last decade. Each of these efforts at a seemly female vocation had failed. But in her response to Burke she was not only to find her voice but also the calling and fame that would shape the rest of her short life and inspire women looking for freedom from the cultural restrictions of their time ever since.

Wollstonecraft's pamphlet, *A Vindication of the Rights of Man*, defended many of the ideals that had inspired the American and French Revolutions. It called for a society where aristocratic estates are broken up and given to the poor as equal shares of land, where free trade is allowed to flourish and where people advance by their talents and hard work, not by the luck of their birth. Burke's emphasis on the importance of continuity and tradition are rejected as an excuse to maintain the unjust domination of monarchical and aristocratic elites over the great majority of the rest of the population.

Despite a political ally of Burke famously condemning Mary as a "hyena in petticoats", the pamphlet was a sensation running to a second edition within a few weeks and sparking a controversy, which generated hundreds of pamphlets arguing for and against the Radical vision over the next six years. These included one of the most famous statements of Radical ideals, Thomas Paine's *Rights of Man*. But it also included an even more groundbreaking work from Wollstonecraft's pen with the publication of *A Vindication of the Rights of Woman*.

This astoundingly original volume called for the same rights that Radicals demanded be afforded to men, to be extended to all women. Wollstonecraft called for girls to be offered the same education as boys and for women to be recognised as full citizens. She dismissed the notion, popular at the time, that women were too subject to their emotions to act rationally and called for men to support women in their struggle for their liberty. These ideals were far from accepted by all Radicals but the fact that the book was well received, very widely read and made Mary famous across the continent, says a great deal about how new, small power attitudes were on the rise in the wake of the American and French Revolutions.

However, like many Radicals, Mary was to grow disillusioned with the new French regime as it descended into an orgy of bloodletting and tyranny in a desperate attempt to maintain its paranoid grip on power in the chaos provoked by the Revolution. In fact, Mary saw this terror first-hand, living in Paris for the two years when the guillotine was busiest. Soon, genuinely free thought was being crushed in

France just as the old absolutist regimes around Europe took similar measures to suppress the Radicals who had been inspired by the events of 1789. In fact, the spark that ultimately lit a Radical revolution in Europe came not from the model of France but from the imperial ambitions of Napoleon Bonaparte.

A highly successful military officer during France's revolutionary wars with its neighbours, Napoleon seized power in a coup in the final weeks of the 18th century. He ruled France for the next 15 years by strengthening many of the features of absolutism. The bureaucracy that stretched into every region of the country was enhanced and given even closer ties to central control in Paris. The police force was enlarged and given greater powers with a secret police formed to crush opposition and imprison arbitrarily without trial. The Catholic Church became an instrument of state power and there was no place for parliamentary bodies. And like his absolutist predecessors, Napoleon wanted nothing more than to dominate Europe militarily, politically and economically.

In two ways, however, Napoleon represented a highly significant departure from the past. First, his position was not inherited through a noble family line nor was it based on divine right. Napoleon drew his power solely from his control of military force combined with the appeal of a vision, which foresaw a world created in the image of the French Revolution. The Civil Code, which he established as the new legislative framework for France, proclaimed all equal before the law, the end of feudalism and aristocracy, and freedom of religion.

Second, Napoleon also inherited from his immediate revolutionary predecessors a new type of military, of which he made full use in his ambitious wars across Europe. In 1793, conscription was introduced, creating an armed force one million men strong. The professional standing army of the absolute monarchs was replaced by the mass citizen army.

In these ways, Napoleon represented the emergence of a new type of governmental big power: the dictator backed by the hard force of the army and police and the soft force of an ideological mission. It was a model that was to prove incredibly influential, reaching its zenith in the middle of the 20th century under the fascist and communist dictators of that period.

In the shorter term, however, Napoleon's influence was to provoke Europe into a new phase of the battle between big and small power. His military prowess and the overwhelming force of the French citizen army meant that by 1810 he controlled Spain, much of Germany and Austria, northern Italy including Rome, the Balkans and Poland. He swept away monarchies and aristocracies and replaced them with bureaucracies, mass armies, constitutions and their own dictator who, more often than not, was a member of his family.

Some across Europe and in America welcomed the invading armies, seeing them as a liberation from absolute kings and feudal aristocracies. But the reality of Napoleon's rule did not live up to the revolutionary billing. Defeated nations were forced to pay vast sums as punishment for resisting Napoleon's forces, taxes increased and the methods of the French secret police were employed against any opposition. Maybe worst of all, the French citizens' army became increasingly European, with forced conscriptions across the continent. Of the 600,000 men Bonaparte used for his ultimately doomed invasion of Russia only a third were French.

Soon rebellions against French rule began to spread, particularly in Italy and Spain. Equally importantly, the Radical sense of national and individual freedom began to re-emerge. Napoleon and the French Revolution had promised freedom and equality but all they had delivered was foreign domination and exploitation. However, Bonaparte *had* destroyed the old regimes of absolute monarchs, so thoughts naturally began to turn to throwing off the rule of the French deceiver and replacing him with genuine freedoms rather than simply returning to the old autocratic dynasties.

But this spirit was to butt up very firmly against the plans of the big European powers. Despite the agitation across Europe, Napoleon was ultimately defeated, not by rebellion from below, but by the massed armies of Britain, Austria, Prussia and Russia. The victorious powers rearranged Europe as they saw fit at the Congress of Vienna in 1815. A core principle of the settlement agreed there was that monarchs should be restored to their rightful place at the head of Europe's nations. Kings were returned to France, Spain and southern Italy; northern Italy was handed back to the Habsburg monarchy in Austria and the pope's power was restored in central Italy.

This effort to return the continent to a period before the French Revolution condemned Europe to a century of turmoil and conflict. The European population of 1815 was not the population of 1715. The small power ideals of the Radicals had already been popularised. America was looked to as a model by increasing numbers. A growing class of merchants and entrepreneurs and newly confident groups of students and intellectuals no longer felt any allegiance to the old monarchies and their talk of divine right, which now seemed hopelessly outdated.

Gradually over the next 30 years the values of national self-determination, limited government, elected parliaments and basic rights such as free speech, religion and assembly, grew in popularity. Radical ideals and the reactionary machinations of the great powers inspired revolutionary societies, which became major movements and sparked occasional riots and rebellions against the imposed monarchs during the 1820s and 1830s across Europe. Even England, which had the weakest monarch and most powerful parliament, and had not suffered absolutist rule since the mid-16th century, saw campaigns emerge demanding extension of the voting franchise and civil rights.

The Radicals consciously built large grassroots movements organising huge demonstrations, mass petitions and even indulging in assassinations of monarchs and officials that stood in the way of change. A younger generation of Radicals forged links with the emerging labour movement, which sought better working conditions for the rapidly growing and largely impoverished urban working class.

This long foment finally caught fire in 1848. An uprising in Sicily in January demanding a constitution, inspired similar action across the continent so that by the summer much of Europe was in a revolutionary state with mass protests, barricades, riots and even armed combat in France, Italy, Germany, Austria, Hungary, Poland, the Balkans and Romania. Gains were made rapidly with many governments agreeing to constitutional change in the hope they could take the heat out of the rebellions and save their skins. King Louis-Philippe of France was overthrown and a republic declared. In Rome, the Pope lost all the authority he had outside the Church, as a new Radical government took over. In a move that would have warmed Madison's and Wollstonecraft's hearts, the pontiff's lands were confiscated and handed out in equal portions to the peasantry.

However, just at the moment of their greatest victory, the Radicals fell apart. A more moderate wing of the rebels called for the revolutionary acts to halt and urged compromise with the existing regimes. Others wanted to press on and sweep away all monarchy, religious hierarchy and aristocracy. Soon this "springtime of the peoples", as 1848 became known, descended into chaos, division and petty political manoeuvring. The old regimes spotted their opportunity and through forging alliances with the moderate rebels, and in some places old-fashioned, violent suppression, regained control in the name of order just as the absolutist monarchies had after the turmoil of the Reformation.

TWO SOCIALISMS

The ultimate disappointment of 1848 spelled the end for the Radical movement that had begun with the American Revolution. Out of its ashes emerged two new forces. The first were the liberal parties that now took advantage of parliaments granted by monarchs during the revolutionary uprising to secure influence and power. They very gradually managed to extend the franchise and introduce moderate legislative reforms inspired by Radical values.

The second was the socialist movement. Working-class self-organisation had been around for many decades but as the industrialism of the 19th century took shape, the numbers working in the modern factories and living in crowded cities began to grow rapidly. The failure of 1848 persuaded many working-class activists that Radicalism, which had always been led by middle-class intellectuals, no longer offered a way forward.

A new emphasis was now placed on establishing new organisations led by the workers themselves and which would use their power as the labour behind modern industry to bring about change. Intellectually, there was also a shift away from the Radical focus on free trade as a liberating ideal and towards notions of collective ownership.

However, there was little agreement even in these early days of what a socialist society would look like and how best to achieve it. Many divisions, intellectual and organisational, permeated the movement. One of the most intense was that between those who believed socialism could be delivered by democratic, peaceful means and those who favoured revolutionary uprising, violent if necessary. Another, often overlooked today, was that between what the political theorist, Paul Hirst, has called associational socialists and collectivist socialists.

The associational strand's first and maybe greatest thinker was the French writer and activist Pierre-Joseph Proudhon. Proudhon shared with other socialists a belief that modern industrialism was exploiting the working classes. Like them he turned his back on the free trade ideal of the Radicals and the more moderate Liberals, which he believed was just an excuse to enrich the property owning classes at the expense of the workers.

Proudhon felt the route to an egalitarian society controlled by and for the workers was for those workers to establish their own autonomous organisations. These would be run in a democratic fashion and the wealth they generated would be shared out equally. In common with other associationalists, he stayed true to the Radical hatred of hierarchy, orthodoxy and elitism.

Proudhon's vision remained inspirational to many for the next five decades. Socialist thinkers, activists and politicians such as J.N. Figgis, Harold Laski and G.D.H. Cole continued to develop Proudhon's ideas, arguing for a socialism that valued diversity and autonomy alongside equality and workers' liberation. At the heart of the vision, however, was always the ideal of democratic organisations controlling a nation's wealth in the interests of the workers rather than the capitalists.

The associationalists felt they were on strong practical ground in the late 19th century. At that time, the socialist movement was centred not on political parties (particularly as most working people had yet to secure the vote) but on workers' and consumers' co-operatives, trade unions and the friendly societies which provided welfare, insurance and other forms of support for working people. To many this seemed the future of socialism.

By contrast, the "collectivist" strain of socialist thought was far more concerned with delivering greater economic equality for working people and had less immediate interest in the old Radical ideals of autonomy and diversity. These, the collectivists argued, were middle-class values.

For thinkers like Karl Marx, and particularly for his followers, the goal of socialism was to win state power, seize the productive assets and wealth of a nation and use it on behalf of the workers. Many felt that the only way to do this was through revolution and probably armed conflict. But as the franchise was extended as a result of liberal influence in parliament, many socialists began to wonder if there was also a democratic route to gaining control of the state.

Whether it chose a revolutionary or democratic route, however, collectivist socialism differed fundamentally from the associationalist approach. The former may have been committed to the idea of building a mass grassroots movement to deliver change but ultimately that movement was there to support the work of an elite using the top-down power of the state to change the world. The elite could be the leadership of a democratic socialist party or the "vanguard" of professional revolutionaries favoured by Lenin who led the Russian socialist uprising of 1917 that established the Soviet Union, but it was always an elite.

Associationalist socialism rejected such top-down leadership. The mass movement they envisaged was one of practical change in the here and now with working people establishing their own organisations or, more radically, seizing those controlled by capitalists. Change was not to be delegated to charismatic leaders or a political class, nor was it to be deferred to some point in the future when an election could be won or a revolution launched. Transformation would happen organically and maybe somewhat chaotically as workers acted on their own initiative to change their world on their own terms.

The associationalist vision was bound to lose favour by the early 20th century as big power ideals came back into fashion. As Paul Hirst says, the associationalists did not want for powerful ideas but they "could make little headway against the notions that centralisation and the large-scale (were) the most efficient and historically inevitable ways of organising social relations".

Ultimately, and certainly ironically, socialism, which had its origins in the small power vision of 18th and 19th century Radicalism, would become the major ideological force behind the big state in the 20th century.

It was a long way from the ideals of James Madison.

6

Government Gets Very Big

In 1913, the US Congress debated the introduction of a tax on income. The proposal was for a 1% tax on all earnings and a 6% tax on any income over $500,000. When the necessary legislation was passed, after an epic political battle requiring a constitutional amendment, one influential congressman predicted the tax "would produce more money than the mind of man would ever conceive to spend".[4]

Fast forward a century and most people in the USA now hand over around one quarter of their income in tax while earnings over $400,000 attract a rate of close to 40%. This shift towards a big state was one of the defining features of the 20th century but it had its origins in the final decades of the 19th century.

Public spending rose as a proportion of the whole economy from around 10% to 13% between 1870 and the 1910s in all industrialising economies. This shift may seem trivial now but it was widely commented upon and analysed at the time. Some of the rise was due to increases in military spending – a role for the state well established by the absolutist monarchs. But there

---

4   Public spending and tax data in this chapter is from Vito Tanzi, *Government Versus Markets: The Changing Economic Role of the State*

was a major new element to the growth: urbanisation. As populations moved from the countryside to seek work in the new industries springing up around towns and cities, governments felt themselves under pressure to respond to two new challenges.

The first of these was to undertake expensive public works such as building sewerage systems, transport links and communication networks required to make the expanding cities work properly and allow domestic business to compete with foreign industry.

The second, and much more significant for the long term, was to provide support for those who could not support themselves or find work. The extensive networks of family, community and church that had provided such care in rural settings were largely absent from the new urban environment and it was widely felt, rightly or wrongly, that the state had to fill the gap. As a result, governments in the late 19th century started raising taxes in a limited way to spend on services such as orphanages, insane asylums, homes for the elderly, limited healthcare and limited education.

Although the rise in the size and activity of the state was very small compared to what was to come later, the principle was gradually being established that governments had a role beyond that which had been accepted for many centuries of maintaining the security of the nation, protecting law and order and upholding established religion.

A much more significant growth in the size and power of the state was to occur in the first half of the next century. Tax levels in most advanced economies rose from between 10% and 13% of the total economy in the 1910s to between 25% and 30% in the early 1960s. Public spending followed course with a rise from an average of 13% of the total economy just before the First World War to an average of 28% by 1960.

While these figures capture the stark reality of the rapid and unprecedented growth in the rise of big government, they don't catch the shift in mindset that went alongside it. For much of the 19th century it was very widely accepted that the state could either not change society's problems or that it would make them worse if it tried. This was a world in which those who argued for a bigger, more powerful state were looking to revive absolute monarchies or the empire of Napoleon. Those who saw themselves on the side of human and civil rights and, increasingly, democracy, rejected such visions.

During the 20th century, however, this view shifted very radically. The big state became associated not just with authoritarian and reactionary views but also came to be seen as an ally of liberal causes and democracy itself. Among a growing number of intellectuals and politicians, big government was regarded as a precondition for human progress with an ever-expanding faith being placed in the power of government to run an efficient, logical and fair economy and society.

As a result, by the middle of the century, the state had not only radically expanded its taxation and spending to provide large scale healthcare, social security and education services, but in much of the advanced world it also had a very powerful role in regulating economies, intervening in its citizens' daily lives and even owning and running vast monopoly businesses in key sectors such as energy, transport, telecommunications and heavy industry.

WHY DID THE BIG STATE GROW SO RAPIDLY?

There were three factors that drove this remarkably rapid shift in opinion and practice in the space of just three or four decades.

WAR

The earlier half of the 20th century was scarred by the two biggest and bloodiest military conflicts in history. The First and Second World Wars were not like previous conflagrations which had generally involved relatively small armies fighting a series of pitched battles. These were so-called "total wars" that involved the mobilisation of the full industrial might and human resources of one nation against another and which saw no target, civilian or military, as out of bounds. Such conflict required a huge effort of central co-ordination and, needless to say, was extraordinarily expensive. As a result, both wars required the state to take on a bigger role than ever before in directing not just the military effort but also ensuring that all of a nation's resources were being adequately directed towards securing victory.

At one level, this simply meant a very significant rise in public spending. Three years into the First World War and public spending as a proportion of the whole economy had risen above 70% in Germany and, remarkably, above 100% in France. Some of this was paid for in higher taxation but all of the combatants also relied very heavily on borrowing: a fact that was to have a devastating effect on postwar economies, particularly in Germany.

Although taxation and spending did fall back after both conflicts, it never returned to its position before the war. So in Britain, state spending as a proportion of the whole economy rose from 13% before the First World War to 45% during it, but only fell back to around 25% after peace returned, where it stayed roughly until the outbreak of the Second World War. Spending then rose during that conflict to over 60% of the whole economy and then fell back after 1945 to around 35%. In effect, the two World Wars had allowed the UK government to more than double the amount of money as a proportion of the economy it had to spend. An unprecedented shift in the space of just 30 years and one replicated across Western Europe.

In some part this is explained by the fact that the costs of war did not end with the signing of peace treaties. Total war took a uniquely high toll on human life and economic infrastructure. As a result, governments were landed with long-term bills to support the families of killed and wounded servicemen, to rebuild housing and factories, deal with enormous refugee populations and, of course, to pay off the vast debts accumulated by funding war efforts.

However, something more subtle also occurred. War made big government more acceptable. The established 19th century objections to high tax and spending could not be sustained at a time of national emergency, and when the war was over they emerged substantially weakened. A "new normal" had been created in which the public and intellectuals were generally willing to accept higher taxes and spending.

Even more significantly, war revealed what big, hierarchical state co-ordination could achieve. It showed, supposedly, that central planning and leadership could drive a united nation to extraordinary industrial output, amazing innovations like splitting the atom, unmanned flight, the jet engine, numerous medical advances and ultimately, in the case of the Allies, victory over a foe who had appeared invincible in the early years of the Second World War. Many became sure that a similar level of central co-ordination and united effort could secure huge outcomes in peacetime as well.

THE STATE'S NEW SKILLS

This interest in a bigger state and the growth of government itself was also driven by the fact that for the first time in history it was simply possible for the state to take on such a significant economic and social role. For the whole of human history the great majority of the world's population had been spread out thinly across rural areas in small villages and towns. Transportation and communications rarely travelled faster than the speed of a horse. The only way central governments could assert their authority on a daily basis was to rely on the loyalty of local officials or nobles.

By the early 20th century this situation was changing rapidly. A telecommunications revolution led by the discovery of radio waves and the use of the telegraph meant governments could keep track of what was going on in the furthest reaches of their sovereign territory and issue orders to its local officials in a matter of minutes instead of days or weeks. Speedier transport in the form of the railways and then cars and planes also made it far easier for states to despatch resources and humans at great speed in response to crises and disorder, or just to ensure the efficient running of public services.

The co-ordinating power this new technology gave to governments was only strengthened further by the fact that ever larger numbers were leaving the countryside to live and work in urban areas, often in the employ of big corporations. Millions of citizens were now concentrated in cities, making them ever more easily observed and controlled by central government.

These cities gave rise to a new mass culture as the patchwork of traditions, languages and customs of rural life gave way to something more homogenous. Governments were quick to exploit this as well as the new mass communication technologies of radio, cinema and then television, to encourage support for state activities and obedience to its regulations. This top-down control of mass thought and behaviour was taken to its greatest extreme in the totalitarian regimes of Nazi Germany and the Soviet Union but democratic governments were not averse to enforcing certain norms through the mass media in the middle of the last century either.

What is often forgotten, however, is how the changing nature of work and the economy made the big state possible. Throughout history, the great majority of people worked the land, providing just enough food for themselves and their families and handing over any surplus to their superiors in the form of harvested produce. This made taxation very difficult. The majority earned too little to have anything significant to hand over to governments, and even when they did have enough, that wealth was usually held in the form of perishable foodstuffs, which was clearly of limited use to governments that needed hard cash to fulfil their objectives.

This began to change rapidly in the 19th and 20th centuries. The rise of manufacturing companies and then the expansion of the large corporations brought millions into paid employment for the first time. In addition, those manufacturing companies were creating a much larger economy built around cash and trade rather than the barter and subsistence of the rural economy. Many were lifted out of rural poverty and, over time, into the comfort of urban living. Substantial numbers now had money to spend on food, shelter and clothing and had some left over to spend elsewhere.

This meant governments in the advanced economies could, for the first time in history, tax relatively easily by requiring cash earnings to be handed over. And they could do so without necessarily forcing their populations into poverty and hence provoking disorder and rebellion, as was repeatedly the case in pre-industrial times.

THE RISE OF DEMOCRACY

The third factor contributing to the growth of the state was the rise of democracy. In the final years of the 19th century and the early years of the 20th, the vote was very considerably extended in many advanced economies, particularly in Western Europe. As the right to vote was gradually widened to less wealthy citizens, the UK saw the percentage of households where the male head of the family could cast a ballot grow from just 4.2% in 1867 to 74.2% in 1911. By 1920 most countries in Western Europe had universal male suffrage. Many extended the vote to women in the following decade and by the mid-1940s women's suffrage was almost total in Western Europe.

This gradual but reasonably rapid shift towards mass democracy changed the dynamics of politics very significantly. For the first time, the less well-off and the outright impoverished had a formal and persistent voice in politics. Demands for the state to deal with issues like poor housing and working conditions as well as the hardship faced by the unemployed, the elderly and the ill grew in strength and importance. Politicians had to respond to these demands if they were to be elected into power by the growing electorates of Western Europe.

This new electoral power also changed the perspective of working class voters and leaders themselves. By the 1910s, socialist parties had been established across the continent. These parties proved extremely effective at attracting the votes of the millions of newly enfranchised workers now employed by the large corporations and living in cities and large towns. Soon they found themselves in government or, at least, as major groups within national parliaments. This changed the focus of working-class movements from the practical, local efforts of associationalist socialists, towards governmental programmes to alleviate hardship, which inevitably involved raising taxes and increasing public spending. In a largely doomed effort to avoid electoral oblivion, even many liberal parties also moved to the left embracing some if not all of the elements of the socialist vision of a bigger state.

BIG STATE THINKERS

This combination of total war, the new capacity of governments to tax and control their populations and the growing political power of working-class movements inspired a dramatic shift in attitudes in intellectual circles. Mainstream opinion in the 19th century still identified the big state with the mercantilist and militarist values of the absolutist monarchies and Napoleonic dictatorship. A small state, which allowed individuals, trade and innovation to flourish, was widely regarded, certainly by the second half of the century, as a precondition for human progress. But the changing conditions of the early 20th century created a great intellectual shift: a bigger state making rational choices rather than the self-interested decisions of the old dictatorships gradually became accepted as a major driver of human progress. None epitomised this emerging Big Power Consensus better than John Maynard Keynes.

Keynes' fortune was his huge intellect. At the age of 13, he won a scholarship to Eton, Britain's most prestigious private school with fees that usually would be beyond even the comfortable income of his father, a university professor. At Eton he excelled in every subject. His brilliance got him elected to "Pop" – an elite club for the brightest and best within an already highly elitist school, which as a rule educated the children of aristocratic families rather than middle-class low-borns like Keynes.

A further scholarship at Cambridge beckoned to study maths where Keynes fell in with another elite group. The Apostles was a group of freethinking aesthetes, which was ultimately to form the core of The Bloomsbury Group of writers and artists of which Keynes was an enthusiastic member. This highly liberal circle also allowed Keynes to explore his bisexuality and indulge his life-long love of art in all its forms.

Like his father, Keynes was soon lecturing at Cambridge University in economics. His perspective reflected the mainstream opinion of the time. Like so many others, he followed Adam Smith's highly influential views that the state should, as a general rule, leave the economy alone to trade, innovate and grow.

However, like millions of his generation, Keynes was transformed by the First World War. He secured an influential role in the Treasury and began to see for himself that new world of total war where states actively plan economies for a specific end. His experience of the poverty, economic volatility and unemployment that followed the war sealed the shift in his economic outlook.

Having already gained fame for his strident criticism of the Treaty of Versailles, which demanded large-scale reparations from a defeated Germany, he was soon attacking the Conservative government of the 1920s for their traditional economic policies.

Apart from the Liberal Party, which was, by that time, in serious electoral decline, Keynes' views had little influence. Two events changed that. The first was the Wall Street crash of 1929 and the severe global Depression that followed, creating large-scale unemployment in the UK and across the world. The second was the publication in 1936 of Keynes' masterpiece, *The General Theory of Employment, Interest and Money*, which not only rethought mainstream economic models, but also provided a rigorous case for the argument that governments must actively intervene in economies at times of recession.

Put very simply, Keynes argued that the mainstream idea that free markets always ultimately find a near-perfect state in which as much employment as is possible is offered, is wrong. In fact, Keynes claimed, at a time of deep recession the very opposite can happen. Because economic confidence is damaged and because everyone is simultaneously paying off debts rather than buying and investing, economies can stagnate for long periods of time, leaving resources unused – a fact that was most noticeable in the long lines growing outside labour exchanges and welfare offices. Indeed such images only added to the suppression of what Keynes called the "animal spirits", which in normal times encourage people to invest and buy.

Only one institution had the resources and power to escape this self-defeating cycle: the state. It alone could take the decision to spend, which businesses and individual households would find impossible at a time when everyone else was being so cautious. As a result, and completely contrary to much received economic wisdom, Keynes called on governments to do the opposite of a recession-hit private business, and spend more than they secured in revenues. The gap would be filled by borrowing from financial institutions desperate to lend at cheap interest rates.

That would mean running a deficit and accepting rising public debt for some time but, as Keynes pointed out, as the economy returned to health thanks to the state-led stimulus, tax revenues would soon pick up, allowing the debt to be reduced and the books to be balanced. The alternative could be years of stagnation with no prospect of growth and higher employment or improved tax revenues.

Keynes' greatest immediate influence was in the US when President Roosevelt responded to a downturn in 1938 by accepting the idea of the government running a deficit to inject $5 billion into the economy. This was a significant shift in Keynes' favour. The New Deal policy launched in 1933 also invested public funds to stimulate the economy but had been designed to ensure that the government's books always remained balanced (in theory at least).

But it was World War II that elevated Keynes to the status of all-conquering economic guru. Just as with the First World

War, the Second further enhanced the popular and intellectual acceptance of the idea that states can control economies for the public good, and that high levels of borrowing, taxation and spending were normal.

Towards the end of the war, the notion was enshrined for the UK in a paper produced by the government, which committed the state to maintaining "high and stable" employment by raising public spending when necessary through accepting short-term deficits. It was a Keynesian document through and through that explicitly rejected the orthodox view that the economy would rebalance itself if it was simply left alone.

The landslide election of a Labour government in 1945, who, unlike their Conservative opposition, ran on a determinedly Keynesian programme, cemented the economist's influence. And despite his early death at the age of 62 in 1946, Keynes' impact was completed in 1951 when the Conservative Party accepted the broad thrust of many of the policies of the Labour Party.

In the US, Keynes took longer to have such a powerful influence. President Eisenhower specifically rejected Keynesian economics despite an economic slowdown in the 1950s. It was not until the Democrats took over the Presidency in the 1960s that the sort of economic policies that were influential in the UK became so in the US. Again, consensus emerged rapidly with the Republican President, Richard Nixon, declaring himself a Keynesian in 1971.

More than any other figure, John Maynard Keynes secured acceptance for the idea that the state can play a vital role in correcting the inherent flaws of a market economy and that it can do this, effectively, by making itself bigger and more influential through public borrowing and spending. In this sense, he was a giant in the rise of the Big Power Consensus during the 20th century.

OWNING THE ECONOMY

Two other policies grew in popularity after 1945, which also expanded the state's role. These are often wrongly associated with Keynes, who was primarily concerned with the economic role of governments at times of recession. Those policies were the nationalisation of private companies and the expansion of the welfare state and public services.

The notion of the state acquiring and merging many private firms was particularly practised in the UK and to a lesser extent in France. The 1945–51 Labour government created huge state owned monopolies or dominant firms in coal mining, electricity generation and distribution, gas supply, iron and steel production, telecommunications, railways, airlines and healthcare. Together, these firms employed no less than two million people. France followed a similar path, nationalising coal mining, gas and electricity generation and distribution.

As the historian of British economic policy, Jim Tomlinson, has pointed out, the reasoning behind this very considerable expansion of the state was confused, ambiguous and overloaded with objectives. For some in the Labour Party and wider trade union movement it was simply a way of ensuring decent pay, working conditions and harmonious industrial relations. Some saw it as a method to address the long-term concern that UK financial institutions did not invest enough in corporate innovation and growth to compete with the big US firms.

For others, however, nationalisation was very much part of the Big Power Consensus. With the state controlling the investment decisions of such sectors, the goal of regulating demand to prevent recession and unemployment was, supposedly, that much more achievable. The Keynesian belief that governments could invest in the short term to avoid joblessness and wasted resources was radically extended. British and French governments introduced a permanent change to the structure of key parts of the economy, which greatly enlarged the power and influence of the state.

The fact that such a significant shift could occur without much clarity on its goals says much about the way the Big Power Consensus had taken a grip of political thinking during and after the war. The idea of concentrating economic power both in vast single corporations and in the state appealed because it fitted a zeitgeist, which saw planning by expert central authorities as infinitely preferable to the chaos and unpredictability of the market and individual choice. The supposed result would be a stronger, more efficient economy made up of more secure, better off people.

THE STATE: YOUR LOVING PARENT

Not many democracies shared the UK's obsession with state ownership, but one common feature after the war was the continuing expansion of the welfare state and public services, which had begun their gradual growth in the late 19th century. By 1936 public spending in the UK on education, health and social security payments had grown from 2.6% in 1900 to 9.16% of the whole economy. Over the next 30 years it continued to rise, reaching 15% by the mid-1960s. A similar if less extreme pattern emerged in the US with social security payments growing from 1.61% of the whole economy in 1940 to 4.69% by 1965.

As mentioned above, this expansion of the role of the state in providing welfare and services to its citizens was driven in part by a strong popular view that after the severe sacrifices made by whole populations during the war, there could be no return to a world scarred by the hardship of the Depression years. Citizens who could be called upon to lay down their lives for their country had a right to expect a basic standard of living and care should they fall on hard times or face ill-health.

But other factors also explain the rise of centralised state provision of public services and welfare. A strong paternalist mentality gripped intellectual and political thought. It was pithily and famously summarised by the Labour MP Douglas Jay in his highly influential book called *The Socialist Case.*

. . . housewives as a whole cannot be trusted to buy all the right things, where nutrition and health are concerned. This is really no more than an extension of the principle according to which the housewife herself would not trust a child of four to select the week's purchases. For in the case of nutrition and health, just as in the case of education, the gentleman in Whitehall really does know better what is good for people than the people know themselves.

This faith in the wisdom and superior insight of experts and professional administrators helped legitimise grand postwar schemes which saw themselves as giving elite professionals the resources and structures they needed to improve people's lives, whether that was in healthcare, education or employment. This aspect of the Big Power Consensus helps explain why the new public services and welfare systems that were set up were usually so hierarchical, in which due deference always had to be paid by staff and by the users themselves to their more knowledgeable and better educated superiors.

As explained above, the big, state-centred nature of the new structures was also possible because the associationalist strand of thought which had been influential within the working-class movement since the early 19th century had been forgotten. It is telling, for example, that the Beveridge Commission – the

1942 government inquiry that recommended welfare state and public service expansion – was overruled by Labour leaders in its call for a decentralised health service run by local democratic structures and the communities they served. Equally telling is that William Beveridge's follow-up report published in 1948, which explained how voluntary and community action could provide for people's needs beyond the most basic care he felt should be provided by the state, was largely ignored.

THE BIG STATE: ANTI-COMMUNIST WEAPON

There was also an element of Cold War politics behind state expansion after World War II. Many political figures were deeply fearful of the growing power of communism. When the fighting stopped, the Soviet Union was in an infinitely stronger position than it had been in 1939. Stalin now had effective control not only over Russia but also the new communist regimes he was forcibly installing in most of Eastern Europe and a large part of Germany. The Eastern Bloc's military power and supposed economic vibrancy and efficiency was lending great credibility to the communist cause. As a result, communist parties across Europe and even in the US began to grow and exert influence, particularly within the trade union movement. Increasingly in continental Europe, communist parties with close allegiances to the Soviet Union were also winning elections.

The large-scale expansion of state provision was regarded by more moderate socialists, as well as those on the right, as a necessary response to the communist threat. In practical terms, preventing hardship simply meant fewer recruits for a radical political movement that hoped to attract those with grievances against capitalism. But in ideological terms it was also important that the Western democracies could show that real action was being taken by political leaders to end hardship and provide for its citizens in ways that communists claimed was impossible. In this way, the Cold War pushed Western nations towards big, centralised schemes that not only mimicked the far more extreme versions of state provision in the communist East but could also be clearly presented as the work of benign Western governments.

THE STATE KEEPS GROWING

What the political architects of this big approach to welfare and public provision never anticipated was that, once established, these centralised, taxpayer-funded systems would just keep getting bigger. While most areas of government spending such as defence, education and infrastructure have either remained static or even fallen, relative to the growth of Western economies, one area has kept on growing: social security and public services. As a result, government spending in Western democracies as a percentage of their whole economies has, on average, risen from around 24% in 1960 to over 40% by 2007. The UK has gone from 32% to 45% and the US from 27% to 37% despite the fact that both countries elected governments throughout the 1980s more committed than any other across the world to reducing public spending and shrinking the size of the state. Consequently, tax revenues have also risen from an average of 24% in 1965 (for all countries in the Organisation for Economic Co-operation and Development (OECD)) to 36% by 2007.

The driving force behind this more recent expansion of the state is very different to that which drove expansion before 1960. The growth in welfare and public service provision in the first half of the century was the product of deliberate choices by politicians usually operating with a democratic mandate to do so. In the last 50 years the growth has been the result of inertia rather than deliberate decision. This may, in part, be the result of the generally higher levels of unemployment that have existed in a more volatile global economy since the 1970s, but the big driver is an ageing population, which has pushed up the government bill for state pensions and for healthcare.

When welfare systems were established, the great majority lived only a few years after retirement. Today, however, vastly improved living standards and better awareness of public health mean that most can now expect to live many years after stopping work. The result is a population that requires pensions for far longer and, as is the nature of older age, makes heavier demands on our healthcare systems.

The result, as the economic historian Vito Tanzi has shown, of this conscious and then unconscious growth in the size of the state, is that from the start to the end of the 20th century, welfare and public services in OECD countries have expanded from around 1% of the whole economy to no less than 25%. As Tanzi says, this is an "extraordinary increase", which "better than any other indicator . . . reflects the change in the economic role of the state during the 20th century".

7

Zombie Politics

The big, centralised, hierarchical state created in the last century is under pressure as never before. The social attitude that accepted its paternalistic ethos has disappeared. The political institutions that run the big state are losing credibility and popular allegiance. The capacity of the big state to deliver what it promises has weakened. And yet governments across the world have barely acknowledged these problems, let alone begun to adapt to them. The Big Power Consensus in politics is remarkably resilient even while new, challenging forms of small power emerge and as populations become increasingly frustrated with a system that no longer matches their aspirations for self-determination.

The result has been a period of extraordinary political alienation and tension exacerbated by the economic problems that began in 2008. Resolving this crisis will require truly profound change to the nature of the state. The massive expansion in state spending, which occurred since the 1960s will need to be reversed. New ways will have to be found to address the healthcare, education and other needs of society. But the way the state works, even a smaller one, will need radical revision to embrace and unleash the small power and creativity of millions of citizens rather than impose ideas from above. First, however, we must understand exactly why the big state is past its expiry date.

THE WEAKENED STATE

The world has changed beyond recognition since the big state structures of the 20th century were established. This change has been detailed with elegance by Moisés Naím, an academic and writer, who was once Venezuela's Minister for Trade, before that country began its own long, self-destructive obsession with big government under the state socialist Hugo Chavez and his successor Nicolás Maduro. Naim shows how three major revolutions have occurred in the last 40 years that have undermined the power of the state.

The More Revolution refers to the fact that there is simply so much more happening than once was the case. We can see this in many different areas of life. The number of sovereign nations has expanded from 67 in 1947 to almost 200 today largely as the result of the collapse of the British and other Empires. According to the United Nations, the number of non-governmental organisations operating across the world to deliver charitable and other services has grown from 6,000 to 37,000 in just the last 30 years.

Alongside this is one of the most remarkable but least commented upon economic facts of recent time: the exponential growth in the number of products and services that now compete for our money and attention and shape our lives in incalculably numerous ways every single day. In three decades, for example, most nations have gone from a mass media dominated by a few major newspapers, radio stations and TV networks, to an uncountable, fluid plethora of information sources communicated via radio, TV and, of course, the internet. Maybe most fundamentally there is the explosion in the global population. There are simply a lot more people than there once were: seven billion today compared with just over two billion in 1945.

This More Revolution is intensified by what Naim calls the Mobility Revolution. People simply move around far more than they used to. There are massive migrations from the countryside to urban areas underway. Those who then live in those urban areas tend to change location more without the ties of family, community and land that once constrained them.

The growing desire for a better and freer life is promoting migration between nations, as well as within them, as vast numbers seek out work, higher pay and the chance to live their lives free of social or political repression. Cheaper international transport and the growth of global networks since the 1980s has created an economy where people are now far more likely not just to travel the world for business and for leisure but to move permanently to places offering them a new job, a better climate or simply a more pleasant lifestyle. And then there is the more recent upsurge in movements of refugees driven in large part by the violent conflicts in North Africa and the Middle East.

The combination of more stuff happening and greater movement makes for a far less predictable and controllable world than the one that existed 100 or even 50 years ago. It is important to remember that one of the big intellectual justifications for the Big Power Consensus, and particularly the big state, was that by concentrating power in the hands of experts and leaders, a much fairer, more efficient, more prosperous world could be created. This was an era of deep faith in planning from above in many areas: the economy, healthcare, education and social values.

That faith in top-down planning and control was misplaced even in the 20th century when the Big Power Consensus was at the height of its popularity. The world was far more complex and unpredictable and uncontrollable even then, but in a world in the grip of Naim's More and Mobility Revolutions the capacity of state officials and their political masters to understand contemporary social and economic trends, forecast their progress and hence take action to shape or channel them in officially sanctioned directions, is that much weaker.

This explains why so much of the political world was completely unprepared for the banking crash of 2008. Despite the existence of highly sophisticated economic models refined over decades by academic departments and government treasuries, despite the establishment across the world of independent financial regulators and central banks, despite the existence of highly qualified and well-paid forecasters and analysts in the world's financial institutions, the crash caught the great majority by surprise. The response of the governments of the advanced economies was one of panic followed by hastily cobbled together bailouts, nationalisations and mergers of the world's biggest banks. Britain's Queen famously asked: "Why did no one see it coming?" The answer is because the world is probably more unpredictable and uncontrollable than it has ever been. The mistake was not to fail to spot the crash but to pretend it could ever be easily spotted and controlled in the first place.

The last of Naim's three revolutions is the most significant. This is what he calls the Mentality Revolution and it essentially mirrors the work of Ronald Inglehart, political scientist and director of the World Values Survey. His rigorous analysis over the last 40 years charts the upsurge of a popular desire for freedom, creativity and self-determination as people begin to take a high level of material security and comfort for granted. This vastly important shift in values has a great impact in many areas but it presents a major challenge to the big state.

The Big Power Consensus generated a climate of public opinion within which populations were more likely to be respectful and supportive of the large, bureaucratic state. There existed a wider, although not universal, acceptance that the people who ran government knew what they were doing and largely had the best interests of the country at heart.

There was also a strong sense that the establishment of the welfare state and major public services had created a new contract between the people and government. After the Great Depression and Second World War, populations had demanded greater fairness in the distribution of material well-being and better care and support from the state for those who fall on hard times. This was now being delivered. The public side of the contract was to knuckle down, get on with working hard and join a shared sense of national mission to rebuild shattered economies. In many ways, it was the wartime spirit continued. In fact, the UK Labour Party ran their 1945 election campaign under the slogan, "And now – win the peace".

As a result of wartime habits, the media remained largely deferential to political leaders and other senior figures. Look back to the political satire of the early 1960s in the UK, represented by theatrical reviews such as *Beyond the Fringe* or TV shows like *That Was The Week That Was* and they appear exceptionally mild by modern standards. At the time, however, they were regarded as hugely daring and even scandalous, generating many public complaints and even discussions within government about an appropriate response. Indeed, the BBC cancelled TW3, as it was known, after two seasons, fearful it was too controversial to run in the election year of 1964. These attitudes are gone. Naim's Mentality Revolution means that populations are far less likely to show high levels of respect to the state and its agencies.

The declining reputation of our political leaders is a strong indicator of this. A 2013 survey conducted by the polling organisation YouGov and Southampton University asked almost 2,000 people in the UK whether they agreed with the following statement: "Politics is dominated by self-seeking politicians protecting the interests of the already rich and powerful in our society". Seventy-two per cent agreed and 8% disagreed. The largest proportion "strongly agreed" at 42%.[5]

The fact that only 8% think politicians look after everyone's interests rather than just the rich and powerful is utterly remarkable, but take a closer look at that survey and something even more noteworthy emerges: everyone feels the same about politics whatever their party allegiance, their age, their gender, their social class or where they are from. There are some differences, but given the scale of disaffection across the board, these are barely significant. Higher social classes are less inclined to agree with the statement but that's still 68% of them compared to 78% for lower social classes. Northerners may be more cynical about Westminster than Londoners but only by 77% to 65%.

Some contend that this shift is nothing new, that distrust of politicians has been around for decades. But recent research does not uphold this view. The University of Southampton has discovered and rerun a survey question that was first asked of UK citizens in 1944: "Do you think that British politicians are out merely for themselves, for their party, or to do their best for the country?" What it found was that in 1944, 36% thought politicians were doing their best for the country, 22% for their party and 35% for themselves. This is hardly a huge endorsement but by 1972 the figures were 28% for country, 22% for party and 38% for themselves.[6] The real collapse in trust has set in over the last 40 years with only 10% believing

5 YouGov *Austerity Leaves Citizens Raging*: http://bit.ly/20RcB65

6 YouGov *Political disaffection is rising, and driving UKIP support*: http://bit.ly/1PfbJr2

politicians put the country first, 30% the party and a whopping 48% themselves, by 2014.

And the picture may be worse than these figures indicate, given that in 1944, and to a lesser extent in 1972, the mass parties had far higher allegiance, so politicians serving their parties' interests might not be regarded as negatively as it is today.

Surveys across Europe and the US find a remarkably similar growth in alienation from mainstream politics and a rise in cynicism towards politicians. A 2013 Harris poll in America, for example, found that no less than 85% of the population believe that, "The people running the country don't really care what happens to them": an increase from just 50% in 2010[7]. Trust in national governments has fallen across the European Union from 34% in 2004 to 23% in 2013.[8]

But something even deeper is changing, as can be seen in changing attitudes to governmental responsibilities. The Role of Government Survey, led by the International Social Survey Programme has been run since 1985. It asks what respondents think governments should definitely be doing. In the UK it has found a consistent drift away from a popular belief that the state should be doing many of the things that the Big Power Consensus established as its important roles.

Providing healthcare for the sick and support for the elderly remained popular in 2006 with 71% and 60% respectively, saying government should definitely do this. Although even for these areas, there had been a drift from 86% and 79% in 1985.

But it is in the areas of economic planning and employment that popular faith in the state's role has collapsed. In 1985,

---

7   Harris Poll *Feeling of Alienation Among Americans Reaches Highest Point On Record: http:// bit.ly/20RcXtt*

8   European Commission *Public Opinion in the European Union First Results December 2013*: http://bit.ly/1RIqAEY

54% thought the state should help industry to grow, 48% reduce income differences between rich and poor, 38% provide a job for everyone who wants one and 45% provide a decent standard of living for the unemployed. The equivalent figures for 2006 were 29%, 27%, 17% and 11%.[9] These are very significant drops. As the political scientist and statistician Paul Whiteley, who has spent his career analysing the ISSP and much other data about changing social and political attitudes said:

> . . . people are less supportive of big government . . . they increasingly expect to support the burdens of old age and sickness themselves, and are less inclined to see government as the sole provider in these areas. The very large reductions in support for job creation, unemployment benefits and the provision of affordable housing together with the drop in support for redistribution suggest that people are less inclined to turn to government to solve their problems. In this respect the role of government has been weakened.

PARTIES WITHOUT PEOPLE

Just as they began to grow in size and power, so our emerging democracies came to be controlled by a new entity: the mass party. The earliest modern parliamentary system emerged in Britain in the 17th century but for around two centuries the electorate remained very small as only those with a relatively high level of wealth were able to vote. Most parliamentary constituencies could be won through the personal contacts of a candidate and often involved bribery and threats to win

---

9   All data quoted in Paul Whiteley, *Political Participation in Britain*

votes. In some areas, the electorate was so tiny that a handful of well-off individuals simply chose one of their number to be the MP.

This began to change gradually with the series of democratic reforms that widened the voting franchise throughout the 19th century. As the electorate grew from thousands to hundreds of thousands to millions, it became impossible for constituencies to be won by a candidate mobilising personal contacts.

Candidates needed money, a professional operation and plenty of local volunteers to reach out to voters. And as citizens began to take their political news and views from the emerging mass media in the form of national newspapers, so a professional national organisation with a clear message was required to influence voters' decisions.

As a result, two mass parties had emerged by the late 19th century to dominate the British political system. These were the Conservative and Liberal Parties. They had growing memberships, a clear set of principles and a clear range of policies presented to the voters at each election in the form of a manifesto. These mass parties were highly structured, disciplined organisations with a single leader, sizeable bureaucracies and large budgets.

That ethos extended into parliament itself. The loose and fluid groupings of MPs with broadly shared values that had shaped parliaments and governments for two hundred years disappeared. Instead, the House of Commons was dominated by two tightly-knit factions, one of which formed the government and the other an official opposition. A system of discipline emerged, known as whipping, to ensure that MPs voted according to the wishes of their leader even if their personal views differed from the party line.

As might be expected given the rise of the Big Power Consensus in the 20th century, this model of the mass party reached the height of its power in the 1950s. In that decade, the two main parties, Conservative and Labour, had approximately three million members between them and secured 95% of the votes cast.

That, however, was the high point. Since then membership and voter allegiance to the two big parties has declined continuously. Between them Labour and Conservative now have only 350,000 members (a 10th of their 1950s level) and struggle to secure around 65% of the votes cast in a general election.[10] In their place has emerged a variety of parties including the Green Party, the Scottish National Party, Plaid Cymru, the Liberal Democrats and the UK Independence Party.

This, in itself, says much about the way voters' attitudes have changed since the era of the Big Power Consensus. The last time there was a similar shift in voter allegiances, one mass party, the Liberals, was replaced by another, Labour. That happened in the early 1920s, but in today's world where a small power mindset prevails, voters turn not to a big party but to smaller forces that can better represent their diverse views.

A similar historical trajectory exists in most other advanced economies and democracies: mass parties formed to operate in an environment of the universal franchise, a period of popular allegiance and mass membership in the middle of the 20th century followed by decline and the emergence of a wider diversity of new parties.

Parties with their hierarchical structure designed to deliver and defend a rigid ideological position and a fixed set of policy prescriptions, covering everything from small business taxation to climate change, cannot offer these small power citizens the influence and diversity they desire.

As election results show, increasing numbers of voters are breaking with the two unappealing party brands that dominate

---

10   Richard Keen, *Membership of UK Political Parties*, House of Commons Library

their political systems but usually as a form of protest with no expectation that their choice will form a government.

So we live now in an era of zombie politics. Our democratic system is shaped around organisations that long ago had the life of popular engagement and support drained out of them. And yet they stumble on, convinced of the good work they do, putting voter disengagement down to apathy, completely oblivious to the fact that most voters look on them with disgust.

There has been an irrevocable shift in the nature of the state and in our attitudes to it. No longer can governments claim the knowledge and power required to plan our world. And we no longer think they should be planning our lives in the way they once did. However, our political systems have failed to respond to this new world of self-expression and self-determination in anything like a thoroughgoing fashion.

Does this mean the state is dead? Or that democracy is heading for the rocks? Not at all, as long as the old elitist, hierarchical systems can adapt to a new era of small power values. Two radical shifts in the way our democracy works and in the way our governments spend the money they take from us in tax are central to this adaptation.

8

Let Us Have Our Say!

The establishment of democracies across the world in the 20th century was one of the great advances in human history. It was a change that bore an indelible hallmark of the small power ideals of the 18th and 19th centuries: a belief that actions of government should be determined by the values and decisions of its many citizens rather than of a self-appointed elite. However, the modern democracies were established at a time when the Big Power Consensus was at the height of its influence. The result is that those systems still bear two features of the Big Power Consensus that look outdated in our increasingly small power 21st century.

One of those features has already been mentioned: the persistence of bureaucratic, hierarchical, elitist parties. The second is the continuing emphasis on the representative nature of our democracies. It is a core principle of most democracies that the role of the elected members of a parliamentary chamber is to use their own judgement when deliberating about laws and voting on major decisions of state.

Famously, this principle has its origins in the work of Edmund Burke – the great political thinker with whom Mary Wollstonecraft had a bitter exchange regarding radical politics and the French Revolution. Burke was elected the parliamentary representative for the westerly English city of Bristol in 1774. At the time, each constituency elected two MPs and the other successful candidate in the Bristol poll was Henry Cruger, an American-born Radical who had pledged to vote in parliament in line with his constituents' wishes.

In his victory speech, Burke made clear that he did not plan to adopt Cruger's approach. In one of the most famous passages in British political thought, Burke states:

> . . . it ought to be the happiness and glory of a Representative, to live in the strictest union, the closest correspondence, and the most unreserved communication with his constituents. Their wishes ought to have great weight with him; their opinion high respect; their business un-remitted attention. It is his duty to sacrifice his repose, his pleasures, his satisfactions, to theirs; and, above all, ever, and in all cases, to prefer their interest to his own.
>
> But, his unbiased opinion, his mature judgement, his enlightened conscience, he ought not to sacrifice to you; to any man, or to any set of men living. These he does not derive from your pleasure; no, nor from the Law and the Constitution. They are a trust from Providence, for the abuse of which he is deeply answerable. Your Representative owes you, not his industry only, but his judgement; and he betrays, instead of serving you, if he sacrifices it to your opinion.

Burke gives two main reasons for this strongly stated view that MPs should not be bound by the views of voters. First, he argued that making major decisions of state requires deliberation, reason and judgement. These, he argues, cannot be expected of citizens not privy to the careful debates of parliament especially when they may well live up to 300 miles from the debating chamber. Second, he claimed that when an MP is elected he is a member of *parliament* and parliament's job is to act in the nation's single interest, to work for the "general good" not to look after "local prejudices".

As populations grew and the vote was extended, Burke's views only seemed to make more sense. There was clearly no meaningful way to engage the vast multitude in the detailed debates of parliament. More to the point, many of those being enfranchised had very limited education and minimal awareness of the affairs of state. Securing their support for the government through the ballot box was one thing, ran the argument, but they could not be expected to take part in the complex decisions made by statesmen.

WHY BURKE IS WRONG

This is still very much the view underpinning the deep support for Burke's representative principle that exists amongst political classes. Parliamentary representatives generally agree that MPs are better left to get on with their own deliberations and that while they inevitably will seek out the views of their constituents, they should not be required to vote in line with them.

It is a perspective, however, that takes no account of how the world has changed in the last 50 years and hence turns the centrepiece of our democracy into a relic of another era.

It fails to acknowledge that the electorate of today is very clearly not the ill-informed, uneducated electorate of the past. Far from the illiteracy of Burke's time, the vast majority are now educated up to secondary level, and in most advanced economies, very high proportions are educated up to degree level. Information sources about affairs of state are more numerous, detailed and up to the minute than they have ever been. Burke's notion that voters could not be expected to keep up with important political issues because they might live 300 miles from Westminster has never felt more out of date.

Nevertheless, many politicians still contest today that involving citizens in parliamentary decisions would give rise to bad law driven by the ill-informed views of the ordinary voter. This, of course, is the argument that was always used against democracy, then against the extension of the franchise and now against any form of direct influence. The truth is that our elected representatives are also very prone to making bad law, often resulting from short-term media pressure. If representatives were required to encourage and enable deliberation amongst their constituents before coming to a conclusion about how they would mandate that MP, it is more likely that bad law made in haste would be avoided.

Not wishing to sound as arrogant and dismissive as other politicians, some insist that the real problem is that the deliberations of a parliament are too detailed and sometimes too urgent to allow for mass consultation. This is certainly the case but a government's plans for major legislation are always known in advance: deliberating and deciding on a representative's broad perspective on these bills, rather than every clause, is eminently possible. And, of course, if urgent measures have to be taken which genuinely do not allow time for proper deliberation and decision then so be it. Many can, of course, be reviewed, however, at a more leisurely pace.

These Burkean arguments also tend to overlook the fact that not only voters but also MPs themselves have changed since Burke's day. Political parties are now tightly controlled, disciplined organisations. MPs are required to vote with the party line, particularly on issues of the most pressing importance. Those that fail to do so are denied career advancement, face disapproval from their colleagues and may well find themselves the victim of negative, anonymous briefing in the press.

Most, however, never need such sanctions. The unquestioning

loyalty of MPs to their party and its leader means they accept that voting the way they are told is part and parcel of their job. The notion that under such a system, MPs are employing their "unbiased opinion, mature judgement, enlightened conscience", as Burke put it, is clearly absurd. Indeed, as the genuinely independent-minded British MP, Zac Goldsmith has admitted, our parliamentary representatives are often unaware of the legislation on which they are voting, as they simply follow the whips' guidance, let alone having given the issue considered thought.

Some actually believe this tribal discipline is a good thing. They question how stable governments will be formed without parliament being controlled by strong parties and their whips. This, of course, ignores the fact that for the 18th century and most of the 19th century, governments in the British parliament were formed and passed perfectly adequate legislation with very loose associations of MPs. Some of these governments were weak and unstable, some were very strong – rather like our history of governments since the rise of the modern mass party, in fact.

WHAT VOTERS WANT

These outdated big power ideas are one of the main reasons people across Europe and America feel so alienated from our political systems. A 2012 survey of UK voters found that while 64% believe MPs should pay a great deal of attention to the majority view of their constituents when making decisions in Parliament, only 4% actually think they do.

The Hansard Society – a UK body committed to promoting democracy around the world, conducted 14 in-depth discussions with 153 citizens across Britain asking people to come up with reforms that would address their disaffection from politics. The overwhelming majority of reform suggestions "focused on issues of process in terms of how politics is conducted, who should be involved and who should be more influential and who less influential".[11]

Essentially, voters themselves suggest that they want more honesty from their politicians about their performance, a greater direct say over what their elected representatives do and a greater capacity to hold them to account when they fail to deliver. This makes sense, of course, in the context of the weakening Big Power Consensus. As populations become more focused on self-determination and free choice, so the elitist, hierarchical nature of a representative system becomes alienating.

Such reforms inevitably imply some significant degree of shift away from our highly representative approach to democracy based on strong party discipline to a system with a larger element of direct democracy where voters can challenge and shape elected representatives' decisions between elections. One where voters get respected as individuals with a point of view worth listening to, and which ultimately may well shape what their government does in their name.

Still in thrall to the Big Power Consensus, political parties are overwhelmingly hostile to such a proposal. Party leaders and members not only believe that their ideological outlook and policy programme is the only right one but also that their strategy of securing state power and driving change from above is the only route to a better world. Handing real political power over to the voters themselves would require a complete change of approach. It would mean accepting that some treasured policies might well be changed or even rejected by citizens between elections. It would also mean loosening the intense party discipline that now exists, to allow representa-

---

11 Gerry Stoker, *Reforming Politics: Citizens' Priorities*: http://bit.ly/1THTwPG

tives to vote in accordance with their constituents' wishes rather than those of the whips.

THE FATE OF PARTIES

Many believe that such change would mean the end of the political party as we know it. They are fearful that the fundamental role of the political party in a representative democracy will be eroded. That role, as they see it, is to aggregate the views of citizens into one easily digestible programme to be presented at election time and to allow the government to get on with changing laws and taking decisions. There are two things to say about this.

First, political parties do a truly terrible job of aggregating citizens' views. Party programmes are shaped far more by elite discussions within the media, the outdated ideological outlooks of party leaders and members, as well as the obsessions of wealthy donors. Indeed, the fact that membership of political parties has declined so rapidly highlights how limited their direct contact is with the vast majority of citizens and thus how their claim to be a nation's great aggregators is undermined.

Second, aggregation as currently understood by political parties, is based once again on Big Power Consensus thinking. Conglomerating a huge range of policies together into one take-it-or-leave-it programme no longer appeals to voters who have ditched party allegiances along with the catch-all ideologies that shaped thinking in the last century. The secret to political decision-making in a small power era, where people have highly diverse views, is to build consensus and support policy by policy, to get meaningful buy-in day by day and week by week, rather than a sullen nod of the head every five years.

The truth, however, is that even under a more direct system

of democracy, parties will not disappear altogether. It would be for parties that win elections and form governments to set the agenda of legislation and decisions for each parliament. It would be this agenda that the wider public would be consulted upon. At elections voters would be choosing the general political leaning of their MP and thus, assuming that MP's party or association was in the majority, the likely set of issues upon which they would get to deliberate and decide. A right leaning government is unlikely to consult the public on expanding welfare services just as a left leaning one is unlikely to consult on restrictions on trade union activity.

DELIBERATION NOT REFERENDA

This is why a small power vision of direct democracy is not about simply holding more referenda on big issues, as is done widely in many US states and famously in Switzerland. It is about elected representatives rethinking their role, to be the facilitators of deliberations on the big issues facing a parliament within their own constituencies, rather than lobby fodder for their party leaders.

There is a now a vast wealth of experience and technology out there that can facilitate such discussions in ways that allow consensus to emerge from within a constituency. Public sector organisations and others are increasingly using these techniques. Such bodies do not come much more complex than the UK's National Health Service, and yet this is an organisation now developing highly sophisticated forms of online and face-to-face deliberation to shape the decisions taken by the service's executive board.

With this direct and deliberative system in place where MPs are required to reflect the views of their constituents, a representative chamber becomes a very different place. Instead of a rather absurd, adversarial forum beset by tribal point-scoring, it becomes a genuine aggregator of a nation's views. It is an opportunity for representatives truly in possession of their constituents' considered opinions to come and work with their fellow representatives to find consensus and take decisions that they can honestly say reflect the will of the people.

It is often claimed that voters would get bored of the constant consultation involved in a direct system, if they engage with it at all, and that ultimately it would be the self-appointed big mouths and ideologues who got to shape legislation. Leaving aside the fact that our political system is already controlled by self-appointed big mouths and ideologues, this argument could only be made by someone who has never been deeply involved in genuine processes of deliberation that use a combination of new technologies, outreach and carefully selected representative groups, to engage "ordinary people" in big decisions very effectively.

Believe it or not, people actually like to get involved in such discussions when they are conducted fairly and openly and, most importantly, when they think they will genuinely have an impact on the decisions taken by those in authority. This is a small power era when people, far from being bored by it, crave self-expression and influence. Only those with a vested interest in maintaining the big power structures of the last century ignore this.

9

Let Us Choose!

Just as our democratic system is based around the largely unquestioned assumption of representation, so the way government provides public services is also based on a principle that has its roots in Big Power Consensus thinking. This is the notion that the best way to provide services is for citizens to hand over their tax payments and for politicians and public sector professionals to spend those funds on behalf of the service users.

It is a notion that owes far more to the intellectual context within which the state made its significant expansion than it does to the emancipatory, small power values of the 21st century. This *tax and spend from above* principle places vast resources and all the decision-making power in the hands of the elite group of individuals who run our public services. It is underpinned by the very values of elitism, hierarchy and bureaucracy that were at the heart of the Big Power Consensus.

Rethinking this principle is absolutely central to adapting the state to a world where increasingly large numbers demand self-determination, free choice and creativity. It is also vital if public services are to keep pace with the highly complex, unpredictable world detailed by Moisés Naím. The notion that elites can have a grip on all the necessary information and take all the appropriate decisions on behalf of others to maintain effective public services in such a fast moving, fragmented world is clearly unrealistic.

This helps to explain why popular satisfaction with public services is so low. The UK's National Health Service is a striking case in point. One of the biggest employers in the world, funded directly by taxes, notoriously hierarchical, and overseen by the government's Department of Health, based in London, the NHS was the recipient of a vast investment programme in the first decade of the 21st century.

Between 1997 and 2008, spending on the NHS more than doubled from £55 billion to £125 billion per year. Average spending per person grew from £1,168 in 2000 to £1,852 by 2008. Since the turn of the century this huge investment has allowed the NHS to recruit 50,000 more doctors and 100,000 more nurses. There have been rows about how well the money was spent and the impact of other changes but overall one would expect such a major injection of cash and human resources to significantly improve any organisation.

And, in fact, there *have* been real gains. The 1.3 million people on NHS waiting lists in 1998 fell to under 600,000 in 2008. Waiting times for most treatments fell from almost 13 weeks in 2002 to just a month by 2010. Important areas of care such as stroke treatment improved with a 25% reduction in the numbers dying after hospital admission.[12]

And yet popular perceptions of quality over that time did not rise. In fact, a representative survey conducted at the end of this period of growth found that just over one-fifth thought the NHS had got better, slightly more thought it had stayed

---

12   Seán Boyle, *Health Systems in Transition (UK)*

the same and, remarkably, almost half thought it had got worse.[13]

Much like the apparently irreversible rise in dissatisfaction with politics, the problem reflects a deep-seated failure of the organisational principles underlying public services. No amount of investment will change the fact that like our political system, our public sector is simply too hierarchical, elitist and centralised to meet the public expectation for much greater control and free choice over the services they receive.

Repeated surveys by the respected polling organisation Ipsos Mori found that when people are asked what are the biggest problems facing the NHS, the issues of being too bureaucratic and dominated by management is consistently the second biggest issue after resourcing of the service. In fact, this option actually rose in popularity during the period that funding was increasing.

In line with this, when people are asked what gives them a positive perception of a visit to a hospital, the overwhelmingly most popular response is being treated with respect and dignity well ahead of what might be thought of as more basic factors such as cleanliness of wards or even pain control.

And when people are asked whether they think giving them more choice would improve the service they receive, it is should be no surprise that in this age of small power and emancipatory values, the positive response is huge with almost three-quarters in an Ipsos Mori survey endorsing the idea.

Governments have, in fact, recognised this for many years and have responded by incrementally introducing small elements of greater choice and control for public service users. In the UK now parents can, within limits, choose which school their children attend and patients can decide at which hospital they would like to be treated. This replaced established systems

---

13   YouGov, *Labour and the NHS*: http://bit.ly/1Xb6R9x/

where children had no choice but to attend the local school allocated to them by officials, and patients simply had to go where their doctor told them. These have been important steps forward but they hardly amount to a thoroughgoing response to the extraordinary shift towards small power values that has occurred since Naim's Mentality Revolution took hold. However, something far more radical *has* been happening in one corner of public services that offers a guide for small power change.

DISABLED PEOPLES' LIBERATION

For most of the 20th century, people with physical and mental disabilities were treated as cases requiring permanent care, often within large institutions run by medical professionals. The notion that disabled people might want to live independently and determine their own futures like able-bodied people was not considered.

This reflected the Big Power Consensus, which, like many other areas, assumed the professional elite knew best. It was enshrined in the National Assistance Act of 1948 in the UK, which legally required local government to provide accommodation to those supposedly unable to work such as disabled people. Of course, at the time, this was regarded as a great step forward that would prevent destitution and homelessness but it also reinforced the dominant big power view that those at risk needed care from above within a bureaucratic, institutional setting.

Inspired by the radical politics of the 1960s, a small group of disabled people within the 1948 institutions began to develop a different vision. They argued that the main thing stopping them living full lives was not their disability but the very top-down, medical perspective that treated them like incapacitated patients, rather than independent people.

The work of two groups, the Union of the Physically Impaired Against Segregation and the Liberation Network of Disabled People soon inspired vigorous campaigning and activism across the country. These activists then linked up with similar groups that had come to the same conclusions across the world. Huge inspiration was taken from campaigners in California who were establishing new centres run by and for disabled people which valued independence and free choice over care and control from above. Activists began to undermine the big power thinking that shaped their lives and demanded that the institutions that enshrined it were closed down.

However, the most radical step was yet to come. To be truly independent, disabled people needed control of the money that was used to fund the unavoidable help they needed to get around and look after their homes and themselves. However, in a classic example of big power thinking, the 1948 Act specifically made it illegal to hand state funds directly to disabled people themselves. Initially, campaigners persuaded authorities to direct money to third parties operating on behalf of disabled people. The real breakthrough, however, came in 1996 when after much campaigning, the 1948 Act was repealed and for the first time funds could be legally handed over to disabled people themselves to purchase support on their own behalf.

This unleashed a revolution in social care. In the UK and other parts of the world, there has been a major shift in which those who need care are given the option to simply have funds paid directly to them to employ their own carers. Often called "personal budgets", the approach has given free choice and self-determination to tens of thousands of people, who only three decades ago were considered incapable of living outside a medical institution let alone running their own accounts, employing assistants and living in their own home.

The success of personal budgets offers a clear direction for reforming the current big power version of public services. Instead of the default position being a tax and spend from above approach, we need to shift to a system that is based on a tax and spend from below principle or "direct spend". This would mean distributing tax funds directly to the users of services to spend as they see fit.

In education this requires a radical move towards what are widely known as school voucher systems, such as operate in Sweden and Hong Kong and which have been tried in some parts of the US, most famously Milwaukee. Under these schemes, parents are effectively given a completely free choice over which school their children can attend. When the choice is made, the necessary funds to educate the child are transferred to the school by governmental authorities.

However, for small power to operate fully, actual tax funds, rather than a nominal voucher should be transferred to parents to spend. This creates the very direct link between school and parent that is required to give the service user adequate freedom of choice and the necessary sense of control over how their child is educated. Importantly, the parent must retain the power to withdraw their child and hence payment from a school should that school be failing the child. That is far more likely to be the case if parents actually directly pay their taxpayer funded fee to the school on a termly or annual basis. To prevent funds being used for purposes other than educational provision, a digital currency could be employed which could only be spent and received by those with the authorisation to do so.

A similar principle could apply in healthcare. Obviously, for urgent treatment existing *tax and spend from above* is the only realistic option. But where users require ongoing treatment, then a direct spend approach is entirely possible. Given the fact that the need for healthcare can often be unpredictable both in when it occurs and for how long it is needed, a nominal voucher system may be more appropriate. It would be unrealistic and wasteful to load up every citizen's bank account with healthcare funds, which are unlikely to be used, and when they are used, may well need constant topping up.

However, an individual who breaks a limb, for example could purchase, after their initial urgent treatment, their ongoing visits to an orthopedic clinic and physiotherapy unit with a voucher, which would be spent at every trip. If the patient was dissatisfied with the service they received, then they could choose to spend the voucher elsewhere.

The NHS in England and Wales has already taken a small step towards this approach by gradually introducing personal health budgets for people with long-term healthcare needs. Like personal budgets for disabled people, this initiative will give funds directly to patients to spend as they see fit within the health service to best meet their needs. The next step is clearly to apply the same principle to people with relatively predictable but shorter-term needs.

THE SPECTRE OF THE MARKET

Many regard such a shift with horror. Voucher systems and similar schemes are generally associated with attempts to introduce markets into public services. For some, the free choice of the market has no place in services that should be delivered entirely according to need. This is a false objection: there is nothing in offering greater freedom of choice to users that inherently undermines provision according to need. The introduction of personal budgets for disabled people has inevitably faced its challenges, but there is no evidence to suggest that it has undermined the provision of care on the basis of need. In fact, as a system it is far better at identifying the precise needs of users and meeting them. Such resistance is really little more than big power thinking dressed up as egalitarianism: a phenomenon that occurs regularly in the history of the struggle between small and big power.

A more reasoned objection is that enhancing user choice in such a radical form would damage equal access to public services in two ways. First, those better able to navigate the system because of better information or personal networks will use those advantages to get a superior service. So, for example, a middle-class parent will make better use of the free choice available to them to secure a place at a higher performing school for their child because they may well receive advice from teachers they know or simply find it easier to source information on local schools. Second, there is the fear of so-called "cream skimming" where schools or hospitals find ways to select the stronger students or patients with less demanding conditions in order to improve their performance.

To counter these problems it is vital that any shift to direct spend is buttressed by three elements: access rules, premiums and accessible information.

Access rules would require any public sector organisation to provide a service in a completely open way with no selection based on the characteristics of the user. These rules should be rigorously enforced with any failure to abide by such a principle resulting in disciplinary measures or even criminal prosecution. Without such an approach the shift to direct spend is undermined and risks widening the gap between the well off and the less well off. Selection also offers service providers a way to enhance performance other than through innovation and genuine service improvements. For these reasons it would not make sense to allow providers to accept private fees from users seeking to gain access to their service as happens, for example, in some school voucher initiatives in America. That would simply introduce selection on the basis of ability to pay.

Premiums would give those less likely to make optimum use of their free choice greater power within a public service based on direct spend. Particularly in education, poorer parents or those disadvantaged in other ways would be given more funds to spend. This would make them more attractive to education providers meaning those schools would actively market themselves to parents in possession of a premium. It would also mean that schools would be more likely to provide a good service to those parents and their children as their decision to move elsewhere would incur a greater financial loss.

Information provision about the quality of service provided by any organisation would also need to be excellent and easily accessible. Fortunately, the internet has made such information far easier to access and comparison between different providers in the private sector commonplace. In a public sector where user choice has been enormously enhanced, it is highly likely that online services will spring up, which allow easy and detailed comparison between different providers without the need for a great deal of input from public service professionals.

THE QUESTION OF CAPACITY

One of the biggest challenges facing a shift to direct spend is the problem of capacity. In most markets, as demand rises so the capacity of the most popular businesses is expanded through investment. But in the public sector this is more difficult because the amount of money available for investment is limited by the tax revenue available to spend. As a result, there is a risk that the choice for service users becomes restricted. The best performing school or hospital can only take so many students or patients meaning that arbitrary criteria have to be introduced to ration their service such as only serving people from a local area. This forces unlucky users who fall foul of those criteria to go elsewhere. In effect, the service provider begins to act like a monopolistic business that gets to set the terms of its engagement with customers rather than the other way round.

There are three possible ways to resolve this. The first is to gradually increase the amount spent on core services such as education and healthcare at the expense of other government activities such as welfare and policing. This has a logic to it as improvements in the educational achievement and healthcare of a population, particularly among those from lower socio-economic groups, is likely to reduce demand over time for other services which provide a more remedial response.

The second way is to allow private investment in public service provision. This would only make sense if schools and hospitals were able to provide a return on that investment by effectively making a profit. Many find this idea sacrilegious but if it can be shown that it will significantly increase the capacity of public service providers and attract extra investment it would be an effective way of enhancing the choice associated with direct spend.

The third way is to allow a much wider diversity of provision. This gives users a greater choice, meaning that it is less likely that single providers will become oversubscribed. This can be driven by public service professionals themselves being enabled and supported to set up new provision or by groups of users in possession of their direct spend funds grouping together to commission new services jointly. This is effectively the principle behind the free schools initiatives launched in Sweden, the UK, Chile and other countries, which allow groups of parents and nongovernmental organisations to establish their own educational provision.

This ultimately may be the greatest benefit of a direct spending approach. It unleashes the power of service users and providers to act in a highly creative, innovative fashion, broadening the range of services on offer and giving users real choice. In a thoroughgoing direct spend system, for example, users would be free to pool their share of tax revenues to establish consumer mutuals to allow them to purchase services collaboratively and enhance their power within a small power public sector.

With these three reforms to improve capacity, providers from public, private and voluntary sectors would be empowered to establish new services, sometimes quite niche, confident that there is a group of empowered customers out there willing to pay for that service, as well as investors willing to back their initiative, rather than having to rely on the commissioning decisions of top-down bureaucracies. In fact, this is precisely what has happened in the social care sector as personal budgets have stimulated the flourishing of many new enterprises able to offer those requiring care direct help with their daily lives but also advice, information and other forms of support.

Direct spend emerged out of a small power revolution launched by disabled people who rebelled against the Big Power Consensus institutions and values that were limiting their lives. Because of the change they initiated, individuals who were once viewed as nothing more than the subjects of hierarchical and elitist control are increasingly free to live their lives as they see fit. The result is not just happier, more fulfilled people, but greater diversity and creativity in the types of services available to people requiring assistance.

These small power rebels have blazed a trail for all public services. Breaking away from a world where the Big Power Consensus of tax and spend from above goes unquestioned

could deliver the same free choice, better services, more fulfill-
ment and greater creativity in the much bigger areas of health
and education.

The goal must be to take the heretical step of placing real
power in the hands of the multitude of individuals, families
and small organisations, while challenging the inevitable objections from the elites who hold the power already, no matter
how benign and well-meaning those objections appear to be.
That, in itself, stands as a good principle by which to restructure our politics and our public services in line with small
power.

Section III

SMALL ECONOMICS:

TOWARDS DISTRIBUTED WEALTH

10

The Rise of Big Business

THE BIRTH OF THE CORPORATION

In 1786, one big debate raged during the annual election of Pennsylvania's state assembly. The controversy was whether the Bank of North America should be granted permission to continue trading in the state for as long as the bank saw fit.

There was no question about the bank's financial soundness or the legality of its practices. In fact, the business had been given a charter (in effect, its permission to trade) by the federal Congress in 1781 with the firm backing of America's finance minister, Robert Morris, and the strong support of that forceful young representative from New York, Alexander Hamilton. What was in question in 1786 was whether corporations like the Bank of North America should be granted charters to trade at all.

In a debate that foreshadowed the row between Madison and Hamilton some years later, the Pennsylvania Assembly had been deeply divided on the issue in the run up to the election. Leading the charge against the granting of the charter was Representative William Findley. He argued that giving the bank considerable freedoms to trade without regular review by the Assembly would transform the company into a "permanent society, congregated by special privilege" that would allow it to "monopolise economic power and undermine the government because of its large concentrated economic power".[14]

For Findley and his supporters the idea of granting a charter to something like a bank seemed particularly questionable. Charters were usually granted by assemblies to allow civic projects such as the building of a road or the improvement of a port to go ahead – initiatives that were time limited and of undoubted public benefit. What, the opponents of the charter wondered, was the clear public benefit of a bank? Arguments that it would provide cheap credit to Pennsylvanian farmers and artisans left them unmoved. Far more likely, Findley thought, the bank would lend to companies seeking to import and manufacture pointless consumer luxuries while charging high interest rates to ordinary citizens with their precious portion of American land as collateral. The ultimate result would be the gradual concentration of capital and money in the hands of the few who owned and controlled the bank.

After a great deal of debate, the Assembly finally voted 41 to 28 to reject a charter for the Bank of North America. But the election for the Assembly reopened the whole issue. The bank's supporters promised the state's artisans that cheap credit and won the backing of trusted national figures such as Benjamin Franklin. Findley and his supporters were defeated in the election and by March 1787, the bank had its charter.

Pennsylvania was not alone in its wariness of corporations. The concerns of William Findley were replicated in other states and at the federal level. For the later part of the 18th century and the early part of 19th century, America was an economy built largely on small and medium sized businesses mostly rural or artisanal in nature and owned and run by families.

---

14   Quoted in Joseph Blasi, Richard Freeman and Douglas Kruse, *The Citizen's Share: Putting Ownership Back into Democracy*

This was very much a market economy where businesses produced for sale and competed for trade, but it was one without the large corporate interests we now take for granted. The prospect of such bodies seemed threatening to small business and far too similar to the companies that had been chartered by the British monarchy to settle and then control and exploit the American colonies.

However, the pressure for easier and more liberal charters for corporations continued to grow as banks and politicians from Hamilton's Federalist Party saw the economic potential of the large scale investment and production that was beginning to develop in Great Britain with the new technologies of the industrial revolution. A classic example was the effort by a small group of New York City merchants in 1801 – including Alexander Hamilton's brother-in-law – to set up a company that would have the technology and capital to meet the city's entire demand for bread. New York's bakers, however, objected to the plan, protesting its attempts to monopolise the market and its crushing of "the independent spirit". The plan for a New York baking corporation was abandoned. By contrast, an initiative to establish a textile corporation for the City in 1811 *did* secure a charter.

The debate about incorporation of large commercial concerns raged on, as did the variable success and failure of corporations to secure charters. In 1819, however, the US Supreme Court took three decisions that changed the economic landscape forever.

The first was the ruling in favour of the Dartmouth Corporation in New Hampshire. The company, which ran a very lucrative college, was opposed to the demand by the state that it accepted government appointees on their board to ensure it was working in the public interest. By upholding the college's protests, the Court in effect established the principle that corporations have certain rights much like individual citizens to pursue their own interests free of state interference.

Second, the Court established in the same year the principle of limited liability, meaning that if a corporation could not pay its debts it would have to surrender its assets, but the individual investors would not be expected to forfeit their personal wealth beyond what they had invested in the firm.

Finally, the Court ruled that states had no right to undermine federal laws, which were more favourable to corporations.

As the historian and sociologist Charles Perrow, noted, this sudden rush of legal decisions was no "mistake, an inadvertence, a happenstance in history, but a well-designed plan devised by particular interests who needed a ruling that would allow for a particular form of organisation". In fact, the Chief Justice John Marshall had deliberately delayed the Dartmouth case until he was sure there was a secure enough majority in the Supreme Court for the decisions to go the way of the corporation enthusiasts.

For the remainder of the 19th century a series of legal decisions by the Supreme Court and others reinforced the principle that large corporate interests could operate freely without the need to persuade democratic assemblies that they were working in the interests of the wider state or nation. Just as individuals had secured the right to freedom from government interference following the ratification of the Constitution and the Bill of Rights, so corporations had gradually secured for themselves the right to "life, liberty and the pursuit of happiness", a somewhat bizarre development given corporations did not merit a mention anywhere in the Constitution nor the Bill of Rights.

RAILWAYS: THE FIRST BIG BUSINESS

Unsurprisingly, the first part of the economy to make significant use of these freedoms was also the newest: the railways.

Railway building became a mania in the USA in the 19th century. Numerous corporations were set up across the country to lay tracks and run freight services for the nation's growing economy and population. Being a much larger country than the world's most advanced economy of Britain, the US required far more rail. By 1880, the US had 93,292 miles of track, Britain had only 15,563.[15] Thirty years later the US had 10 times more than Britain with almost a quarter of a million miles of national network.

The rapid spread of rail was important for the rise of the big corporation in two ways. First, the speed at which raw materials could be delivered to factories, and commodities to customers, meant that manufacturers with the money to invest could significantly scale up the output of their production processes. Increasingly, the pace of manufacturing was measured in hours as the railway network grew, rather than in the days and even weeks that had been associated with the era of horse-drawn carts and canals. Equally importantly, the railway companies became a model for the new large corporations.

The cost of building and running railways was very high. This was not an endeavour that could be funded by a single entrepreneur drawing on his own or his company's cash reserves, as would have been the norm in pre-corporate days. In fact, costs were often so high that even the pooling of the capital of a few business people (as in the case of the New York baking enterprise) was rarely enough. Instead, more complex and ambitious ways of raising finance would have to be developed, such as making public share offerings and turning to the super-rich families of Europe. As a result, the investment banking industry of New York was established and was almost entirely dedicated to raising finance for railway building between the 1850s and 1890s. Important techniques were

---

15   Charles Perrow, *Organizing America*

developed, which were to be used to grow vast corporations in a wide range of other sectors in the next century.

This also meant that for the first time the people who owned, and the people who managed a business were distinct groups. The European families and wider shareholders who financed the growth of the US railway system obviously had no interest in actually spending their time managing those systems. They were simply looking for a return on their investment. In addition, running a railway company was an extremely complex affair requiring an incredible effort of co-ordination between many different interested parties and literal moving parts. This took experience and expertise. Things investors did not have.

As a result, the corporate hierarchy was first established in the railway industry. A company run by a board of senior directors and investors' representatives (constantly seeking return) with broad oversight of the firm, managing down through a pyramid of managers with increasingly focused operational or local responsibilities. It is a model, of course, that lasts to this day.

ALL THAT MATTERS IS THROUGHPUT

The railways were also the first companies to discover and resolve a central problem of managing a highly complex and costly business. Because running a railway was such a constantly expensive affair, any drop in business and hence income could be disastrous. Like very many corporate interests that came later, railway management was always seeking maximum utilisation of their capacity to keep paying the bills.

This meant that the pressure on railway businesses to keep their prices low was intense. Losing any business to a competitor was terrifying for a firm that needed maximum utilisation and the resulting constant flow of revenue to stay afloat. But low prices limited profits, displeased investors and only ramped up the pressure to maximise throughput. As a result, the railway companies began doing something that was to become a common practice for all sectors of the corporate economy: they looked for ways to keep prices artificially high by reducing competition on price.

This began with informal arrangements between railway firms working on competing and connecting lines to charge their customers agreed rates. These were rarely effective and agreements were regularly broken as one or other firm panicked about throughput and cut prices. So by the 1870s, railway firms were establishing more formal associations, which not only agreed prices but began allocating traffic and even sharing profits according to agreed formulae.

However, the 1870s and 1880s were a period of particularly intense price competition driven by a combination of factors including two financial crashes (caused ironically by the bubble of investment in the railways). Across the world prices were falling and economies were weak for a number of years.

The fastest moving companies with the best access to east coast investment realised that the only way they could now prevent competition was to buy up as many other railway firms as possible. Within a few years, an industry, which had been divided amongst hundreds of firms, was dominated by only 30 corporations running two-thirds of the railway network.

Firms in other sectors that faced similar challenges soon followed the railways' lead. The result was the most intense period of mergers and acquisitions ever experienced by any advanced economy. Between 1897 and 1904 alone there were no less than 2,943 mergers, many involving multiple companies. Over three-quarters of these were so-called "horizontal mergers" where firms competing in identical markets were combined into one company. U.S. Steel, for example, was created in this period out of the merger or acquisition of 785 separate companies.

The mania was only halted when the New York stock exchange experienced yet another financial panic, dampening appetite for further investment in mergers and acquisitions. By then, however, many of the vast corporations which were to dominate the US and global economy during the 20th century had been established: General Electric, Eastman Kodak, American Tobacco, Standard Oil, DuPont, International Harvester to name just a few.

The result was monopoly or near monopoly control in many sectors. By the early 1900s, American Tobacco controlled 90% of its market, Standard Oil 85% and U.S. Steel 75%.[16] Just 100 firms owned almost a quarter of all industrial assets in America.

It may have taken a century, but Alexander Hamilton had finally got his way. America was now a nation built around vast, advanced powerful manufacturing enterprises backed by a highly sophisticated investment market based in Hamilton's home city.

THE AMERICAN INVASION

The coming of electrification at the turn of the century greatly enhanced the productivity of these firms, boosting the scale of the corporations even further. This was the beginning of mass production: very large hierarchical corporations using electrical machinery and an extreme division of labour on the shop floor to produce vast numbers of largely identical products at prices that suited the pockets of millions of Americans.

There was an explosion of firms producing goods for this expanding consumer market, most famously symbolised by

---

16   Patrick Gaughan, *Mergers, Acquisitions, and Corporate Restructurings*

Ford's Model T – the first motorcar that could be afforded by someone on a reasonable salary. The variety of new firms created by this boom led to yet another merger wave after 1916, which ended in the most severe financial crisis in history, with the Wall Street crash of 1929. Again, some of the best known and most dominant corporations were created at this time: General Motors, IBM, John Deere and Union Carbide.

The growth and success of American corporations inevitably caught the attention of the wider world. By the early 20th century, there were strong currents of thought and efforts in business and politics for the other industrialised economies of Great Britain and Germany to "Americanise" themselves.

As early as 1901, the pre-eminent British journalist of the time, W.T. Stead would write a whole book dedicated to the theme called The Americanization of the World. For Stead, Britain's future success lay in emulating American business:

> So far as we can see from the trend of events at the present moment the producing power of Great Britain is likely to undergo an immense increase, because Great Britain is beginning to be energized by the electric current of American ideas and American methods. . . For the last twelve months there has been a constant pilgrimage across the Atlantic from the Old Country, in which our manufacturers, our railway managers, our shipbuilders, our iron-makers, our merchant princes, have been wending their way to the United States for the purpose of learning the secret by which the Americans are beginning to beat us in our own market.

Stead, however, did not see the coming of the First World War. This caused massive disruption to industry across Europe, and the economic and political turmoil that scarred the inter-war years made it very difficult for British and German business to imitate the American corporation in any sustained fashion.

In fact, a heavyweight committee set up by the UK Government in 1931 to explore the challenges facing an ailing economy concluded that British business was seriously handicapped by the nervousness of British banks to copy their New York counterparts by launching large-scale investment in new business ventures and growth.

The result was a so-called "American invasion" with the large and wealthy US corporations taking advantage of the smaller, less technologically advanced European businesses, to expand into their markets, particularly once Europe entered a more peaceful period after 1945. Between 1917 and 1948, the number of American manufacturers with subsidiaries in Britain rose from 22 to 93, but by 1971 this had grown to 544. While in Germany, US subsidiaries rose from 14 to 33 between 1913 and 1953 but reached 330 by 1971.[17] Not all sectors were affected by this US expansion, but those where large scale delivered really major advantages, such as food, chemicals and machinery, became heavily dominated by what were rapidly becoming multinational corporations.

The influential French journalist, Jean-Jacques Servan-Schreiber, wrote an enormously successful book about rising American corporate influence in Europe in 1967 called *The American Challenge*. The book sold 600,000 copies in France and was translated into 15 languages. Its opening passage states:

> Fifteen years from now it is quite possible that the world's third greatest industrial power, just after the United States and Russia, will not be Europe but Ameri-

---

17 Alfred Chandler, *The Visible Hand*

can industry in Europe. Already in the ninth year of the Common Market, this European market is basically American in organisation.

Were he alive W.T. Stead would no doubt have been deeply disappointed to read this. But Servan-Schreiber seemed unaware of the shifts in European industry. The Americanisation of domestic industry that Stead had expected at the turn of the century was actually beginning to happen in a sustained fashion by the 1950s, uninterrupted by war or economic depression.

With the help of US consultancy firms, most notably McKinsey, and by recruiting American managers, European companies finally began to adopt the big approach, integrating and merging separate businesses or business units under a hierarchical, centralised management structure, adopting mass production systems on the shop floor and expanding overseas; ultimately even challenging American firms in their own domestic market.

This led to another period of intense merger and acquisition activity during the 1960s as large companies sought to deliver returns to their ever-hungry investors in a more competitive global economy. However, the law against monopolies in the US (more about this later) made it difficult for firms to repeat their trick of buying out direct competitors, so this was a period when well-established companies working in one sector bought up successful firms in other sectors creating a new type of giant, centralised, hierarchical firm: the conglomerate. A firm like ITT, which had operated as a telecommunications company for 40 years, suddenly started expanding its corporate model into sectors such as car rental, hotels, consumer credit, construction and even baking, in a wild bid to keep generating super profits for their backers on Wall Street. The result in the US was over 6,000 mergers during the 1960s, which saw no less than 25,000 firms disappear into the arms of vast conglomerate corporations.[18]

The early fears that the corporation would mean vast swathes of economic life falling under the control of a new elite running large hierarchical structures were completely vindicated. The diversity of companies and the consequent smaller scale of those firms and the wider distribution of economic power that characterised early capitalism in Britain and America itself were destroyed by the merger mania of the 1890s and then the spread of the corporate organisation overseas to Europe after the Second World War.

Equally importantly, the mindset of the world shifted in this time. Despite the concerns of men like Madison and Findley being justified, their perspective was largely forgotten during the 20th century. Success bred its own universal admiration. America had gone from being a largely rural and artisanal economic backwater in the mid-19th century to producing over a third of the world's industrial output on the eve of the First World War – more than the share of the world's two other great economic powers, Britain and Germany, combined.

As the words of W.T. Stead and others like him throughout the 20th century show, it was the American corporation's size, managerial skill and sheer power to invest vast sums in growth and development that was seen as crucial to the country's startling economic success. If it had not been for the turmoil of economic crisis and two world wars then it is likely that the big, concentrated, hierarchical American model would have been adopted much earlier outside of the US. By the middle of the century, however, the economic version of the Big Power Consensus was in place.

18   Patrick Gaughan, *Mergers, Acquisitions, and Corporate Restructurings*

11

Big Economic Power Challenged

THE CHIEF ECONOMIST'S DREAM

As a symbol of the last century's love of big business and big government, you could not do much better than the UK's National Coal Board (NCB). Created in 1946, it merged 850 private mining companies into one massive corporation owned entirely by the British state. At its height, the NCB controlled over 1,600 mines, possessed more than a million acres of land and employed 700,000 people. Much of Britain's industry relied on coal, so the NCB and hence the government were at the very heart of the country's economy. In terms of scale, importance and (literally) power, the NCB was big – very big.

But in 1960, the NCB's chief economist started to have a strange recurring dream. He would be sitting in the board-room with all the organisation's directors (as he had done regularly for the last 10 years) discussing matters of grave importance to the coal industry and the wider economy. The directors would intone seriously about a problem before identifying a solution, after which one of the members of the board would walk over to a large telephone switchboard and start plugging wires purposefully into various holes to implement the decision. After a while, the chief economist would feel compelled out of curiosity to explore this device. What he always found was that the machine was connected to nothing at all.

These surreal imaginings might be dismissed as little more than a vaguely interesting anecdote from the depths of British industrial history, were it not for the fact that the economist in question was a German émigré called E.F. Schumacher, the author of a book read by millions, including student radicals, academics, business leaders, and presidents in the mid-1970s. The work was called *Small is Beautiful*.

For much of his life, Schumacher followed an intellectual road travelled by very many economists in the 20th century. As a young man he had been schooled in, and largely accepted, the conventions of technical and conservative mainstream economics. During the 1930s, however, he fell increasingly under the spell of John Maynard Keynes.

Schumacher came to believe that the state had a central role to play in directing and planning a nation's economy. Like many of the time, Schumacher was convinced that such planning would address the instability and inequality of capitalism while also using the vast concentration of resources and power available to governments to deliver a more efficient and innovative economy. With such convictions, Schumacher was perfectly placed to take on the chief economist role at the NCB.

However, around the time he started having that dream, Schumacher broke with the script. To the utter bewilderment of his colleagues and friends, this man, brimming with intellectual self-confidence, began to question the very principles around which he had built his career and which underpinned the economic policy and business practice of the time. As in his dream, Schumacher was discovering that the great things promised by big government and big corporations amounted to far less in reality. When he finally summarised all of his thoughts in *Small is Beautiful* in 1973, he found a world enormously receptive to his ideas.

The book sold rapidly, was translated into many different languages and Fritz Schumacher was quickly booked up for speaking engagements across the world. He was showered with honorary degrees and awards.

Technology was the central issue for Schumacher. He was passionately concerned that in its furious pursuit of all things big, businesses and governments were placing creative and meaningful work beyond the grasp of ordinary people. Because politicians and business leaders had become so enamoured by the power and profits that resulted from huge concentrations of resources, a giant technology had been created to satisfy that desire. Massive factories contained enormous, complex machines and processes that churned out millions of standardised products. Humans had become the slaves of these machines working to the remorseless rhythm of the factory.

Establishing a small-scale business, which a worker could run on their own terms and employ their unique creativity, had become impossible because the investment required to purchase the technology used by big business was way beyond the means of the ordinary person.

Schumacher was scathing about how meaningless private property becomes when its ownership is available only to the vast corporations that he had seen grow in power and wealth over his lifetime:

As regards private property the first and most basic distinction is between (a) property that is an aid to creative work and (b) property that is an alternative to it. There is something natural and healthy about the former – the private property of the working proprietor; and there is something unnatural and unhealthy about the latter – the private property of the passive owner who lives parasitically on the work of others.

Private enterprise carried on with property of the first category is automatically small-scale, personal, and local. It carries no wider social responsibilities. Its responsibilities to the consumer can be safeguarded by the consumer himself. Social legislation and trade union vigilance can protect the employee. No great private fortunes can be gained from small-scale enterprises, yet its social utility is enormous.

It is immediately apparent that in this matter of private ownership the question of scale is decisive. When we move from small-scale to medium-scale, the connection between ownership and work already becomes attenuated; private enterprise tends to become impersonal . . . The very idea of private property becomes increasingly misleading.

Schumacher was unclear about what could be done to save the advanced economies from themselves now they had travelled so far down the road of big power, but the developing world, he argued, had time to choose a different route. He spent much of his later life travelling the world trying to persuade the governments of Africa, Asia and Latin America to adopt what he called an "intermediate technology" approach. Rather than mimic the mass production economies of the capitalist West and Soviet East, which pulled millions of workers off the land into dehumanising and destructive work, developing nations should adopt a different technology that would allow the masses to set up their own small businesses and workshops in their own communities. This technology would aim to be more productive and geared to a modern economy than the spinning wheels and anvils that had been around for centuries, but it would not replicate the giant, complex machines and processes so beloved of the West. Schumacher was fond of quoting Gandhi's maxim: "Not mass production but production by the masses".

Hugely overworked through endless travel, lectures and meetings with the powerful, Fritz Schumacher died suddenly on a train travelling through Switzerland on yet another speaking tour. He was 66 and it was just three years since the publication of his masterpiece. Maybe he should have slowed down a little, not just for the sake of his health but also to take stock of what was actually happening in the most advanced economy on the planet. *Small is Beautiful* was wildly popular in America where Schumacher's lectures attracted thousands of young people looking for new answers to the questions posed by the rebellions of the 1960s. He even earned a personal audience with President Carter. But Schumacher was unaware that it was values very similar to his own that were inspiring a small band of Californians to create the intermediate technology that the economist thought he was more likely to find in the rice plantations of Burma and the backstreets of Delhi.

THE HOMEBREW REVOLUTION

During the 1960s the big corporate model of which Schumacher was so critical had taken a new turn. It had become computerised. The enormous complexity of managing the vast administration, production, marketing and distribution efforts of the biggest companies the world had ever seen required an ability to control information that was beyond the capacity of mere humans. Computing firms like IBM and Honeywell came to the rescue. They rapidly became highly successful companies themselves, providing the superior information management corporations required. They also found eager customers in government, which needed similar levels of data control to manage the enormous military, welfare, health and other functions now delivered by the state.

As Schumacher recognised, organisations built around great concentrations of power and resource would demand technologies designed to suit their big model. True to form, the technology developed and deployed by IBM and others was built around a vast computer, which did all the memory and processing work for an organisation. This computer could be accessed and manipulated by terminals that had no major processing power of their own. This was computing mimicking and reinforcing the Big Power Consensus – it was expensive, centralised and complex.

However, in January 1975, a magazine called *Popular Electronics* carried a front cover story about a new computer called the Altair 8800. It was a remarkable machine. It used the most advanced microprocessing chip on the market and was priced at only $397. Most importantly, however, it was a home terminal – it could be used without being attached to a massive, centralised mainframe computer.

The computer was designed and manufactured by a company called MITS and its CEO, Ed Roberts, was praying that the publicity generated by *Popular Electronics* would lead to at least 200 sales and save his company from the bankruptcy it was facing. Roberts' prayers were answered many times over – within a few weeks the company had 4,000 orders. MITS had tapped into the early stages of the small power revolution.

But there was something hollow about the Altair 8800; literally in the case of the model displayed on the front of *Popular Electronics*. MITS had only managed to produce one working model and that had got lost in transit to the magazine – what appeared on the cover was nothing more than a metal box. Staff worked frantically to meet the orders but still customers had to wait months for their computer.

The Altair was also strictly for tech fanatics. It took days to piece together, hours to programme and then could only do the most basic tasks such as flash red lights in a certain order. And, with no memory, the results of any programmer's efforts were immediately wiped as soon as the machine was turned off.

As a sustainable product, the Altair was hopeless and MITS was gone within four years, but it did act as a catalyst for one of the most important blows against the Big Power Consensus. This was the rise of home computing which created the infrastructure for the development of the technology, which, more than any other, would make the 21st century an era of small power – the internet.

Although the early home computing pioneers could not foresee the internet, they did understand very clearly that their mission was a revolution against big power. Lee Felsenstein was a case in point.

Introverted, short-haired and with no interest in drugs, he was an unlikely student revolutionary. He was enough of a leading activist, however, for the defence attorney in a notorious trial against the organisers of an anti-war demonstration to have called for Lee to be on the stand instead of his clients.

For most of his revolutionary comrades, computers were part of the problem: incomprehensible machines that were used by corporations, the military and government to enhance their control over information and bulwark their power. But Lee didn't agree. Computers were indeed used by big power for their own ends, but he had the knowledge, being an electronics engineer, and the vision to realise that computers could be used to free people, if only those people could get access in the first place.

Lee Felsenstein was not alone. Although the intersection of the Venn diagram sets labelled student revolutionary and computer geek was not large, it was big enough for some of its members to find each other. After placing an advert in the back of a radical newspaper, Lee soon found himself working with a handful of like-minded people calling themselves Resource One. To Lee's frustration, the group did little more than talk.

But that was before Ted Nelson wrote and self-published *Computer Lib* in 1974. Here was a manifesto, a call to arms that sent a jolt of electricity through the rarefied and niche world of tech revolutionaries. Nelson proclaimed "cybercrud" as the enemy: the false ideology that kept the use of computing power restricted to a powerful elite working for big corporations and big government. As Nelson wrote:

> Knowledge is power and so it tends to be hoarded. Experts in any field rarely want people to understand what they do, and generally enjoy putting people down. Thus if we say that the use of computers is dominated by a priesthood, people who spatter you with unintelligible answers and seem unwilling to give you straight ones, it is not that they are different in this respect from any other profession. Doctors, lawyers and construction engineers are the same way. But computers are very special, and we have to deal with them everywhere, and this effectively gives the computer priesthood a stranglehold on the operation of all large organizations, of government bureaux, and everything else that they run. It is imperative for many reasons that the appalling gap between public and computer insider be closed. As the saying goes, war is too important to be left to the generals. Guardianship of the computer can no longer be left to a priesthood.

Fired up, Lee took Nelson's call to deliver "Computer Power to the People" very literally. Abandoning Resource One, he worked with a new group called Community Memory to develop terminals that would be placed in public spaces for use by anyone.

The most successful effort was outside a hip record store in Berkeley called Leopold's. As Community Memory explained in a handout, the "Model 33" was an attempt to create "a communication system which allows people to make contact with each other on the basis of mutually expressed interests without having to cede judgement to third parties". The terminal was immediately popular.

Many people searched for basic information – the addresses of health clinics in Berkeley, advice on good places to eat, contact details for plumbers. All the results printed out on paper, as monitors were still in development at this time. But then visitors to the record store started leaving random messages for others to see: "U.S. get out of Washington", "Let a smile be your umbrella", "1984 will find you".

Users also began to have more detailed conversations about government domination, often stimulated by the long, slightly paranoid entries by a mysterious figure calling himself Dr. Benway. One user wanted to know where the best New York style bagels could be bought in the Bay area. It got four responses. Three gave addresses of bakeries. The fourth came from someone called Michael who had a radical suggestion – give him a call and he'd show the inquirer how to make their own bagels.

So primitive forms of data searching, tweeting, blogging and peer-to-peer creativity were already underway within a few days of the public's first exposure to an accessible computer. The tools of a small revolution were being forged. And Community Memory was not alone, across the US but particularly in California, a growing number of individuals and informal groups inspired by Ted Nelson were taking action to drag computers away from big power and give them to "the people".

It was into this dynamic world of experiment that the Altair 8800 was launched and it explains why, despite its many flaws, it was received with such unexpected eagerness. The Altair was not just a machine – it wasn't even simply a new and exciting generation of existing technology. It was regarded as an instrument of liberation – the first step on a road that would lead to a completely different world where big power had lost control of the flow and generation of information.

The machine was studied intently at the very first meeting of one of those informal groups: the Homebrew Computer Club. Without the Altair, the club may never have got past the 32 people who attended that meeting in a Menlo Park garage but with it a fire was lit. Suddenly there was focus to their activity: building new hardware and writing software to make the Altair into something vaguely useful. And when the severe limitations of the Altair and MITS became clear, there was an even more stimulating goal – building a better machine.

Within weeks, Homebrew was attracting hundreds. It became clear that something significant was happening. Revolutionary ideas about society combined with revolutionary ideas about technology at just the right moment to bring together, as one member put it, "the damned finest collection of engineers and technicians that you could possibly get under one roof". And there was little doubt (or modesty) about the likely impact according to the same Homebrewer: this was the "equivalent of the industrial revolution but profoundly more important to the human race".

And, of course, Lee Felsenstein was at the heart of it. Although he had not helped found Homebrew, he was soon its convener and master of ceremonies. It was the making of the man. The introverted technician, who had the reputation among his 1960s comrades for never laughing, became a skilled, engaging and witty facilitator of what could well claim to be the most important hobbyists' club in history.

Lee shaped the burgeoning group to be a mix of informal and formal interaction with opportunities at every meeting to share information, ask technical questions, view presentations on new developments and then, maybe most importantly, network like mad. Homebrew directly inspired and supported people at the earliest stages of their careers, who were to become central figures in the home computing industry. It spawned a variety of companies and initiatives some of which went on to success but many of which provided vital lessons in how not to do things in this new world.

Maybe most importantly, it became the context within which the fertile mind of a computing engineer called Steve Wozniak was stimulated. Inspired and informed by the discussions at Homebrew, Wozniak was determined to create the best home computer he could – not one for geeks but one that could be used by anyone whether they understood how it worked or whether they couldn't care less if it was powered by a microchip or a potato chip.

Wozniak soon teamed up with Steve Jobs – a man with far more business than computing sense. The result was the production of the first genuinely reliable home computer that could be used by anyone. This was the Apple II. It was launched in 1977. Within a few years Apple was a multimillion-dollar business with tens of thousands of their computers populating offices, schools and homes. The big computers for big organisations model was dead. This was Fritz Schumacher's "intermediate technology" happening for real. The small economic revolution was underway.

THE OBSCURE AUSTRIAN

At exactly the time Fritz Schumacher was having his strange recurring dream, Fritz Hayek was getting used to obscurity. Better known as F.A. Hayek, the austere, tall, snuff-taking Austrian economist had trod a very different path to his German namesake. Unlike Schumacher, Friedrich Hayek had never been seduced by the ideas of John Maynard Keynes – quite the opposite. For a brief period in the 1930s, just as the Big Power Consensus was taking hold, Hayek led the intellectual opposition to the emerging emphasis on the big state.

With Hayek based at the London School of Economics (LSE) and Keynes at Cambridge University, a rather ill-tempered and often highly technical row broke out between the two institutions. For a few years, it seemed an even match, but Keynes' influence in government, enormous international standing and, some might contend, greater skill with complex economic analysis, won out.

An academic colleague, Ludwig Lachmann, explained ruefully that when he arrived at the LSE in the early 1930s, "everybody was a Hayekian; at the end of the decade there were only two of us: Hayek and myself". All the others had defected to the Cambridge perspective. Keynes, of course, was also far more in tune with the strengthening Big Power Consensus. Hayek looked, sounded and thought like a relic from another age.

Hayek, however, burst back with a vengeance in 1944. His fearsome attack on the love of state power and control exhibited by the extremes of both left and right – *The Road to Serfdom* – was a rapid and unexpected worldwide bestseller. It hit the right note just as fear of fascism was being replaced by fear of a new totalitarian menace in the form of the Soviet empire across Eastern Europe.

But the book also carried a much more controversial message. Hayek claimed that the growing trend towards economic planning in the West – inspired by his old Cambridge adversary – had within it the seeds of the very totalitarianism that Britain, the US and their allies had just shed much blood defeating. In the end, it was this unpalatable and frankly exaggerated claim, which ensured that Hayek's fame was short-lived. The popularity of social democratic parties across Europe showed that the fears of *The Road to Serfdom* were not widely shared by voters. For a second time, Hayek had flirted briefly with influence and fame but had then faded.

Hayek's opposition to the big government vision of Keynes and his supporters was rooted in the fundamental principles developed by a group of economists based in Vienna, where Hayek had studied as a young man before coming to London. For this Austrian School of Economics, an economy was fundamentally about the generation of value – the production of things that had worth. But this begged the question that had obsessed economists throughout the 19th century: what exactly gave a commodity value? Many economists of the time such as David Ricardo and Karl Marx felt it was the human labour expended to produce it.

The Austrian School, however, had a very different answer: value is whatever a consumer judges it to be. This so-called "subjectivist" position essentially meant that the value of a product was unknowable until it was offered for sale. Before a product's value became clear, millions of consumers had to make their own complex and highly individual assessments not just about the product but about the product relative to all other products that might take their fancy. Ultimately, the outcome of all those assessments would be revealed through the price they were willing to pay.

For Hayek and his dwindling band of allies, this was what Keynes with his big government mindset overlooked. The economy was unimaginably complex, essentially unknowable in its day-to-day details and, most importantly, all the more successful because of that. Price was an astoundingly effective way for millions of consumers to tell producers what they valued at any particular time. The result was an economy that was far from perfect but one that did ensure things got made and were distributed to the right people at the right time and in the right quantities. To believe that such a spontaneous, complex and efficient system could be bettered by the planning of a small group of intellectuals and bureaucrats was a "fatal conceit" as Hayek entitled his very last book.

However, Hayek's analysis was not simply a counter to the big state vision that so seized the world in the 20th century. His approach was an impassioned plea to let the small decisions and value judgements of millions of individuals flourish without interference from above, by concentrated forms of power. Indeed, as time passed and Hayek continued to labour in the wilderness, he turned away from technical economics and developed into a philosopher who tirelessly developed his core belief that the spontaneous social organisation that emerges from the small decisions of millions of individuals are not only more respectful of human dignity and freedom than big centrally planned systems but are also more efficient.

Hayek was no anarchist or radical libertarian. He believed that the freedom and efficiency that arises from spontaneity only does so because everyone follows clear and universal rules about how they interact. These are the rules that ensure people trade fairly and openly and respect each other's private property. They needed to be constantly adapted to changing circumstances by elected lawmakers. They also needed to be enforced by the state. But importantly, they were decidedly not laws designed to restructure society or shape the details of human behaviour in a way decided by politicians. They were simply the clear rules of a game that provided great freedom for the players to make their own decisions and interact in diverse ways.

Hayek hoped that his monumental study of these rules – *The Constitution of Liberty* – would prove to be his masterpiece and a worthy successor to *The Road to Serfdom* when it was published in 1960. However, despite some good reviews, the book did not sell particularly well, nor did it generate any public interest. It looked as though both Hayek and his ideas had been defeated by the tide of history. Soon, the Austrian professor succumbed to a decade of ill health and depression in which he wrote little.

In 1974, however, something expected by no one, least of all Hayek himself, happened – he won the Nobel Prize for economics. It was a surprising decision by the Nobel Committee. Hayek had been more of a political and social philosopher than economist for over three decades and had been relegated to obscurity for almost as long. It was also a decision that left many mainstream economists – schooled of course in the Keynesian Big Power Consensus – annoyed that such a high profile prize had been awarded to someone whose work they felt had been resoundingly disproved by their guru in the 1930s.

The impact of the prize was huge. Hayek was not only personally reinvigorated, but interest in his work and his views suddenly reached levels he had not experienced since the 1940s. The excitement many felt at the rediscovery of a long-lost thinker was helped enormously by the fact that the shine was rapidly coming off the economic Big Power Consensus. For the first time in 30 years, the twin threats of inflation and unemployment stalked Western economies despite the widespread claims that state-led economic planning had banished these problems for good.

The UK was hit particularly hard. Strikes and demonstrations became weekly events, power cuts disrupted homes and businesses and politicians seemed increasingly helpless. At one stage, electricity was rationed to three days a week to conserve power due to strikes by coal miners. In three short decades, the UK had gone from imperial powerhouse and world war victor to economic basket case. Increasing numbers began to blame this mess on the Big Power Consensus that had dominated economic policy-making since the war. The belief that governments knew how to produce goods better than millions of businesses and their customers was taking a fatal blow to its intellectual credibility.

Ultimately, the popular frustration turned into a political earthquake when two determined politicians – Ronald Reagan and Margaret Thatcher – seized the initiative and decided to overturn everything the Big Power Consensus had said about the benefits of large-scale government. They were both clear about the intellectual debt they owed to Hayek. Famously, Mrs. Thatcher, while being briefed in the mid-70s by a Conservative staffer on the party's Keynesian-lite policies, took out a copy of *The Constitution of Liberty*, slammed it on the table in front of her and declared with typical steel, "*This* is what *we* believe".

Hayek remained an influential figure for the rest of his life, despite his advancing years. Maybe most satisfyingly for him, he lived just long enough to see the collapse of communism in the Soviet Union and Eastern Europe. Thinking perhaps of the decades he spent in intellectual obscurity, he told a friend that he "hardly expected to live to experience this". He died in March 1992 just before his 93rd birthday.

WAS THE BIG ECONOMIC CONSENSUS
ALL BAD?

A good proportion of Deirdre McCloskey's Great Fact occurred in the 20th century. Particularly in the postwar period, living standards rose probably at the fastest rate ever in history. Inequality declined.

This raises an important question: did the Big Power Consensus contribute to this improvement? Rather than small power being the best promoter of human progress, surely history shows that when the corporation and the state are in control of the economy things get much better. Surely Schumacher and Hayek were ignoring the evidence that was all around them.

This argument confuses a coincidence with a cause. Just because big power in business was dominant in the 20th century, it does not necessarily mean that it was the cause of the rise in living standards and equality.

Big power has maintained, and in some senses tightened, its hold on the economy since the 1960s. A smaller number of corporations now control major global markets than was the case in the postwar period and there have been further waves of merger and acquisition mania over the last 50 years. As was explained earlier, the state has grown in size over the same period with public spending as a proportion of the whole economy rising from around 24% in the Western democracies in 1960 to over 40% today.

Yet this period coincides with rising inequality and a slowdown in the rate at which living standards have risen, particularly in the last 20 years. Clearly, big power is no guarantee that the Great Fact will progress uninterrupted.

The truth is there are other factors that better explain the improvements of the last century. First, there were major developments in the labour market at the time. Labour shortages were common in the period after the Second World War. This resulted from the fact that a large number of able-bodied men had either been killed or disabled during the military conflict just as a huge industrial effort was required to reconstruct shattered economies after 1945.

This had two very important impacts. First, it meant that workers could demand higher wages, greatly enhancing the living standards of the less well-off and reducing the differences in incomes between the better paid and those lower down the income scale. Second, as was mentioned earlier, it meant women were positively encouraged to take jobs. This added a second income boost to the households of ordinary workers.

Then there was housing. One great benefit of higher pay was the expansion of home ownership. For the first time, hundreds of thousands of families who may have expected to rent their home in the earlier part of the century could afford to place a deposit on a new house and secure credit for purchase. The supply of housing also grew very rapidly with the construction of new suburbs across the UK and the US, meaning that prices remained low. As a result, many owned a significant asset for the first time in their lives, having a meaningful impact on the distribution of wealth across both countries. This also provided a huge boost to those companies producing goods such as fridges, televisions and other home amenities as the new house owning class rushed to fill their properties with the newest and smartest products. The growth of these firms created a booming economy and even higher demand for workers further pushing up pay.

The greater equality of the last century also resulted from the fact that corporations did not have it all their own way during the 20th century. In the early part of the century in the US, there was a popular backlash against the growth of big business, which resulted in a series of tough laws designed to prevent the rise of monopolies and oligopolies. This anti-trust legislation along with the disruption of the Depression and war prevented any major wave of corporate merger activity across the Western world for over three decades between 1929 and 1965. This meant that while large corporations did dominate the advanced economies very considerably, there was more competition and less oligopoly than there has been in recent years. The result was lower prices for consumers and more competition between the corporations to employ workers, leading to those higher wages.

It is also worth pointing out that the great chronicler of inequality, Thomas Piketty, has argued in his epic work *Capital in the 21ˢᵗ Century* that a very significant reason for the greater equality during the 20th century was because, as he puts it: "The period 1914–1945 was a dark one for all Europeans but especially the wealthy whose income dwindled considerably".

The reason was war and revolution. The vast military conflicts of the time literally destroyed a great portion of the property owned by the well-off, while still more was expropriated by revolutionary states such as those in communist Russia or, more importantly, nationalist regimes that forced out imperial powers across the world. As a result, the gap between the well-off and the less well-off shrank considerably.

However, it would be wrong to suggest that the Big Power Consensus across both business and government bears no responsibility for the reduction in inequality in the last century. Although, it is not as significant as many on the left claim, the establishment of a social security system, more comprehensive public services and higher taxes on the wealthy *did* reduce the gap between different income groups. As another great chronicler of equality and inequality, Anthony Atkinson, has shown, for around two decades after the Second World War, the welfare state played a major role in preventing a drift back to the higher levels of inequality that existed in the early part of the century. After that, however, even its continuing expansion could not stem the rise of inequality. This is one major reason, along with others, why an argument for the abolition of the state is less desirable than its gradual and careful reduction down to levels closer to those seen in the postwar period.

The revolution in ideas introduced by people like Schumacher and Hayek combined with the information technology explosion of the last forty years has ushered in an economy far closer to the small power principles that inform this book. The next three chapters explore what that means in practice and how this small economy can be encouraged even further.

12

Everyone an Entrepreneur

DESIGNER DINOSAURS

When Karli Dendy looked at the visitor numbers on the day she launched her new website, she thought the counter was broken. Karli had expected a dozen or so views at best. In fact, over 10,000 people had come to take a look at her online boutique specialising in dinosaur shaped jewellery.

The reason for the unexpected interest was Etsy. Like a million other entrepreneurs hoping to use the online platform to sell their handmade products, Karli and her boyfriend, Jacques Keogh, had set up Designosaur on the oddly-named arts and crafts website. Karli then tweeted Etsy's team about her new "shop". They retweeted. Suddenly Designosaur was reaching hundreds of thousands of potential customers within the first few minutes of its operation.

Those early views gave Designosaur a great start. It also gave a huge morale boost to Karli and Jacques. But it has taken a lot of hard work and learning to navigate the new world of online small business to get to anything close to stability. The firm started out with just one or two sales a week after it was launched in early 2012 but now makes around five a day. That means Karli has quit the two full-time jobs she needed to pay the rent in recession-hit Brighton on the UK's south coast.

Designosaur is succeeding because of the quality and popularity of the products but also because Karli and Jacques are obsessive online networkers constantly promoting their work through Facebook, Pinterest and, of course, Twitter. They've also built strong relationships with fashion bloggers, some of whom have vast followings and can boost a small business enormously.

The power of this network means the business needed zero start-up capital. The marketing requires no budget because the online networks are free to use even though they can reach a global audience at the touch of a keypad. Stock is largely created as orders come in so there is no need for a bank loan to buy up materials and products and hope the public bites when the final product lands in shops. And Etsy provides all the web space and pages required to show and sell products, charging just a few pence to list items and only taking a commission of 3.5% when sales are made.

Karli and Jacques have no detailed, conventional business plan – why would they when they haven't asked anyone, except their customers, for any money? – but they do live by a simple rule of thumb. If sales decline in one month and they have no idea why or how to respond then they will wind up the business. This is a remarkably exacting standard, which most conventional entrepreneurs would shiver at, particularly those in hock to banks and investors. But as Karli says, things change very fast in the fashion world and even faster in the online fashion world – lose touch even for a few weeks and it's best to get out and start something new.

SCHUMACHER'S DREAM REALISED

Karli, Jacques and millions of other small business entrepreneurs have proved E.F. Schumacher right. He saw that technology at the human scale would unleash the power of private property. It would give people the power to establish their own enterprises, determine their own lives and exercise that deep human need for creativity. This is precisely the world that the radical geeks of Silicon Valley hoped to create in the 1970s and what they have managed to do with remarkable success for the last 40 years.

They refined the personal computer in the late 1970s and early 1980s, leaving the days of the troubled Altair far behind. Initially businesses and public organisations, particularly schools and universities, began to purchase the new technology. As prices dropped and the machines themselves became more reliable, individuals began to buy computers for their own use at home. Gradually, the big mainframe technology began to disappear, plunging IBM – which Lee Felsenstein and his comrades regarded as the great enemy – into a financial crisis.

This IT revolution coincided with the rise of service industries in the advanced economies. Personal computing with its emphasis on the management, production and sharing of knowledge through increasingly ubiquitous Microsoft applications suited a world where sectors such as finance, the creative industries, law and general business services were replacing engineering, the automobile industry, the home appliances sector and mining.

Ironically, because manufacturing moved during the 1980s to the developing world, as cheaper unskilled workers became available there, so change happened in the opposite way to how Schumacher had foreseen and hoped. Asia, in particular, became the new centre of mass production, making highly effective use of big technology, while it was the advanced economies that saw huge change generated by the rise of a smaller scale technology.

That change was stimulated further by the rapid spread of internet use during the 1990s, aided by the creation of the World Wide Web at the start of the decade, which would have been impossible if personal computing had not already been developed and taken up so enthusiastically in the previous 10 years. The lasting outcome of this technological revolution has been the "entrepreneurialisation" of the economy.

THE ENTREPRENEURIAL CONSUMER

The trend began with the shift to wider consumer choice led by Japanese automobile companies, particularly Toyota, in the 1960s and 1970s. The outcome was a great expansion in the variety of goods being sold and the expansion of choice for the consumer.

For example, the number of car models for sale in the US rose by a third between 1982 and 1990, from 151 models to 205. The food industry in the UK introduced 1,030 new products in 1970; this doubled to 2,016 in 1980 and multiplied by nine times to 9,192 new introductions by 1990.

In the US, different brands of cereal rose from 88 to 205 in the 1980s. By the early 1990s, over 20,000 new lines were being introduced into UK supermarkets every year. Brands that had produced only one or two varieties for decades, found they had to generate dozens of products to meet consumer demand. Crest and Colgate between them were producing 35 different types of toothpaste by the early 1990s. Even the new industry of personal computing already had 2,000 models available before mass ownership had taken off.[19]

---

19 Data and sources appear in Adam Lent and Matthew Lockwood, *Creative Destruction*, IPPR

OPEN INNOVATION

During the 1990s and early noughties, companies were beginning to take advantage of the interactivity of the internet to take this explosion of consumer choice to the next logical step: allowing customers to take part directly in the design of their products. This "open innovation" approach has transformed the way many companies do business and changed the expectations of customers.

For over a decade, Proctor and Gamble ran a programme called Connect and Develop, which enabled customers to create new products or improve existing ones. The hugely successful toy company Lego has been an open innovation trailblazer with its Mindstorm range and Design by Me software, which allowed customers to modify and design their own Lego models. Nissan's Project 370Z designed a car online in partnership with customers and motoring enthusiasts across the world. It went on sale in 2015. Many corporations of similar standing – Nike, Converse, Virgin and Starbucks, to name just four – have made open innovation a mainstream part of their business process.

But there are many new companies premised entirely on the concept of open innovation. Threadless is widely quoted as a success story in the fashion world. The firm allows customers to design their own t-shirts online. It then manufactures and sells the most popular designs decided by a vote of visitors to the site.

Thousands of similar firms have emerged: Chocri and Chocomize in the confectionary market; GemKitty, Delusha and Art of Jewels for jewellery; Blank Label and Shirtsmyway in fashion; even the breakfast cereal market has its share of open innovation firms in the shape of MixMyGranola and MeandGoji.

A number of sites also emerged, enabling companies and entrepreneurs to undertake open innovation. The most famous is probably Innocentive, which allows firms to offer cash rewards to those who can solve their knottiest R&D problems, many of which require detailed technical expertise. The site claims to solve one-third of all problems posted.

UnserAller allows companies to work with potential customers in the development of a new product. The site's first project involved 11,000 people in the development of a new range of condiments for a Bavarian food company. Going a step further, Quirky encourages individuals to submit ideas and designs for products. It then develops these, manufactures them for sale and shares revenues with the initiator of the project.

SOCIAL MEDIA

This open innovation trend was superseded in the power they offered to the consumer in the noughties by the rapid rise of social media. Companies such as Facebook, Twitter and YouTube have grown from start-ups to major global corporations with astounding rapidity by creating online spaces where the dividing line between consumer and producer has dissolved almost entirely. Instead of being able to contribute to a largely centralised process of production still controlled or managed by a smaller group or elite, these platforms simply allow millions of users to simultaneously create their own products and consume those created by others.

The rise of this approach has been astounding given social media as a concept did not even exist in the 1990s. Facebook has grown from one million users in 2004 to over a billion today. Twitter from six million in 2008 to half a billion today. This means that in the space of five years between 2005 and

2010 the proportion of internet users using a social media site rose from 5% to over 60%. It stands at over three-quarters of all internet users today.

This shift over the last 50 years, from the mass production of standardised products to ever greater engagement of the customer in the production process, has transformed the nature of the consumer. No longer is the consumer a largely passive recipient of products handed down from on high, exercising power only through the mechanism of choosing to buy one product rather than another. The consumer is now an integral part of the process of generating and adding value to the product itself. In a world where the value of a product is determined by the customer – as Hayek and his colleagues in the Austrian School argued – it makes sense that over time companies have evolved ever closer to the point where the customer actually creates that value for him or herself.

The shift has been particularly impressive in sectors such as the creative industries, journalism and publishing due to the reliance of these industries on the transmission of knowledge and data, which particularly suited the internet. However, it now seems inevitable that with the growing popularity of distributed manufacturing processes such as 3D printing and the increasing ability to control our household appliances remotely and to generate our own electricity, that the same empowerment of individual consumers to shape tangible products is afoot.

Many have noted that this blurs the dividing line between the consumer and the producer to the point where it becomes almost impossible to distinguish between the two. Is someone uploading a popular video onto YouTube a consumer or a producer? They are undoubtedly a consumer of YouTube's platform and tools, but they are clearly adding value to the product of YouTube by creating the content without which YouTube would be unable to attract other customers.

The line is blurred further when one considers that the whole YouTube experience for a user is likely to be a complex interplay of consuming content produced by other users and posting one's own content in response to that consumed content. One need only think, for example, of how popular uploaded clips spawn, without fail, numerous parody clips, which can often achieve as great a popularity as the original video. Under such conditions, the millions who use YouTube are, in effect, engaged in a highly sophisticated, inseparable process of consumption, production and innovation, which confound the conventional categories of business processes.

Few have noted, however, the extent to which these new technologies not only blur the distinction between consumer and producer but also between entrepreneur and customer.

EVERYONE AT THE HELM OF THE SHIP

The dominant view of the entrepreneur in economics comes down to us through the work of Joseph Schumpeter and Austrian School economics. Although Schumpeter was not a member of that school, both shared what might be called a heroic and buccaneering vision of the entrepreneur. In this vision, the entrepreneur is a highly innovative individual willing to take risks by moving resources (such as labour, finance and technology) around in radical ways to take advantage of new opportunities and rapidly shifting market conditions. For both Schumpeter and the Austrian School, this entrepreneurial innovation was the reason capitalism flourished in the way it did, driving forward ever greater improvements in products, raising living standards and improving our quality of life. Indeed, it was the dignity and respect offered to these entrepreneurs that Deirdre McCloskey identified as the cause of the Great Fact.

The leading figure in the Austrian School, Ludwig von Mises, developed a famous metaphor to explain the role of the entrepreneur. For von Mises, the brave entrepreneur is at the helm of the ship directing "all economic affairs" while the consumer is the captain ordering the entrepreneur along certain navigational routes depending on whether they choose to buy a product.

It is a view that still permeates modern culture through popular television shows like *Dragon's Den*, *Shark Tank* and *The Apprentice*, which place the entrepreneur on a pedestal as a type of superhumanly creative, insightful and often belligerent being whose only mortal enemy is themselves when they fail to understand and respond to customers' needs with sufficient speed or awareness.

The shifts detailed above suggest that while this understanding of the entrepreneur certainly contains elements of truth – if overblown and romantic at times – it remains a far too elitist view. The blurring of consumption and production means that entrepreneurial activity is now far more widely distributed.

The use of specialist knowledge and creativity in response to market signals as the defining feature of the entrepreneur is now a skill deployed by many millions rather than an elite group. At its most straightforward this can be seen in the way open innovation processes deliberately employ the insights of the customer to add value to products in order to secure market advantage. The distribution and use of entrepreneurial skills is intensified further by the widening empowerment of consumers to actually produce their own commodities.

Hence, the way content is produced by millions on social network sites and the wider internet in response to complex and often very rapid changes in demand requires just the creative, opportunity-seeking, risk-taking behaviour associated with entrepreneurs. In most cases, of course, such skills are not deployed to generate a financial return but to secure profile or impact quantified very clearly through the metrics used by Twitter, Facebook, other networks and various analytics programmes. However, just as elite entrepreneurial activity generates value in the marketplace and so increases wealth, this wider entrepreneurialism does exactly the same thing for firms like Facebook, even if the wealth does not accrue automatically to the entrepreneurs.

We should not overlook, however, how this mass entrepreneurialism *is* providing new sources of financial revenues for a far wider range of individuals than was the case in the past or as is understood by Schumpterian and Austrian School economists. Just as the boundary between producer and consumer and entrepreneur and consumer is dissolving, so the line between salaried worker and revenue-earning entrepreneur is also increasingly blurred. This further deepens the entrepreneurialisation process being experienced by the economy.

THE ENTREPRENEURIAL WORKER

In the early 1970s, there were around 800,000 small businesses in the UK. This has grown gradually but steadily over the last 40 years to the point where there are now close to five million. The vast majority of these are one person working for themself.

Similar trends have been seen in other advanced economies, but what has been remarkable about the UK experience is that the 2008 crash and consequent recession did not dampen the appetite for self-employment. In America, the supposed home of the enterprising spirit, almost a million workers gave up on self-employment during the recession, but in the UK the figures have kept on growing. It has been estimated that half of all jobs growth since 2008 have been down to people becoming self-employed while no less than 90% of entirely new jobs are people striking out on their own.[20]

Some have tried to explain this shift in the British labour market as a sign of economic weakness. The rise in self-employment has occurred, so it is claimed, because there are so few "real" jobs around. Hundreds of thousands of workers simply feel forced to make a living whichever way they can by securing short-term contracts and casual work.

The data, however, does not support this view. Research by the Bank of England found that the newly self-employed are only slightly more likely to have been made redundant recently compared to the period before the crash. The study also concluded that the self-employed are actually less likely to be looking for a new job than someone in conventional employment.[21]

Nor is there any evidence that the self-employed are unhappy with their lot – quite the opposite. The UK's Understanding Society project, which surveys 40,000 households on a regular basis, found that the self-employed report higher levels of job and life satisfaction than those in conventional work.[22] This is particularly remarkable when one considers that the self-employed do not have access to the benefits that come with standard work such as an occupational pension and regular monthly salary. In fact, the self-employed actually earn less on average than their peers who work for someone else.

In fact, far from the UK's rapid rise in self-employment being a short-term response to economic crisis, it is a result of the deep shifts in workers' mindsets and goals.

That is indicated most clearly by a survey of the self-

---

20 Benedict Dellot, *Salvation in a Start-up?*, RSA

21 Srđan Tatomir *Self-employment: what can we learn from recent developments?*: http://bit.ly/1IZQq3z

22 Quoted in Benedict Dellot and Howard Read, *Boosting the Living Standards of the Self Employed*, RSA

employed in the UK by the Royal Society of the Arts reported in a paper by Benedict Dellot. It asked 2,000 people why they had set up their own business. By far the most popular reason was "to have more freedom" with over half choosing this option while a third chose the second most popular, "to be creative and make the most of a good idea".

Increasingly, employers have begun to recognise the importance of allowing and encouraging autonomous decision-making and initiative amongst employees. This trend started some decades ago with the growing success of Japanese manufacturing firms in the 1960s and 1970s. A large element of that success was put down to the creation of employee teams, which had the freedom to take decisions independently of approval from senior management. This allowed companies to make adjustments to manufacturing processes more rapidly in response to shifts in consumer demand while also enhancing employee well-being.

The enormous success of the IT sector in recent years has strengthened this trend. The tendency of IT firms to break the rules of the conventional workplace while embracing a culture that values entrepreneurialism and speed means that firms like Google are now widely admired as champions of greater employee autonomy and creativity. The notion of "intrapreneurship" – employees acting entrepreneurially within a corporate environment – has, as a result, become an increasingly popular aspiration for many firms.

At the most radical end of the spectrum this has led to the rise of the types of firms explored by Frederic Laloux in his book *Reinventing Organisations*. These do away with intermediate levels of management almost entirely and allow employees near complete autonomy over how they fulfil tasks and respond to shifts in the market. An increasingly famous example is Buurtzorg – a home nursing company in the Netherlands which employs 9,000 nurses working in autonomous teams of 12 but with only 45 people working in the company's central office as managers and back office administrators.

This trend is beginning to show some signs of affecting the wider workforce. The UK's Skills and Employment survey has found a small if significant increase in the amount of discretion employees are able to use at work and in the number involved in autonomous teams since 2006 following a period since 2001 when there was no rise in such conditions.[23]

This entrepreneurialisation of the workforce both within the conventional workplace and through the rise of self-employment is being driven in considerable part by the rise of the internet. The speed of innovation, the millions of micro-shifts in demand or taste occurring every day, and that bewildering blurring of the distinction between consumer and producer created by new technologies means companies must rely on the autonomous, entrepreneurial skills of their workforce to keep up with market developments. This new world of countless niche and bespoke markets opens opportunities for the self-employed and micro-businesses that never existed in the past. The transformatory role played by technology in entrepreneurialisation is only likely to intensify over the next few years.

The so-called "internet of things", which allows machines to communicate with one another will empower consumers to have much more direct control over the behaviour and performance of any machine they use to suit their own unique needs or tastes. This will deepen the rapid, niche driven spirit in existing markets, while introducing it to a whole range of as yet relatively untouched sectors such as food retail, energy and manufacturing. The response from companies will have to be further entrepreneurialisation of their staff, while even greater

---

23   Hande Inanc et al. *Job Control in Britain:* http://bit.ly/1Xb80Ov

opportunities will emerge for the self-employed and micro-businesses.

The roll-out of blockchain technology provides yet more impetus. Blockchain is the highly effective and innovative technology behind bitcoin, the digital currency. It currently allows those receiving bitcoin to be entirely certain that their payment is not fraudulent and that it has not already been spent elsewhere. Importantly, it provides this degree of certainty without the need for any centralised and costly administrative structures as is required by conventional banking and currency systems.

The application of blockchain principles to a wide range of financial services and many other non-financial areas will greatly enhance the capacity of micro-businesses to secure the confidence of customers without the backing of "trustworthy" brands. It also holds out the possibility for much more straightforward online collaboration between groups of entrepreneurs to generate more sophisticated products or services without the need for complex layers of management or contracts to ensure co-ordination and delivery.

THE NEW RIGHT REVOLUTION

Part of the explanation for this shift towards entrepreneurialisation can be found in politics. Hayek's prominence as a philosopher of a flourishing individualism within the context of a free market inspired the New Right movement, which was to secure power in the 1980s in America and the UK. The US President, Ronald Reagan, and the UK Prime Minister, Margaret Thatcher, shared a policy agenda which involved removing regulations on business, selling large state-owned industries into private hands and destroying the power of the trade union movement.

The result was far more freedom for company bosses to

shape their business in line with the financial interests of their shareholders. In the 1980s and 1990s that meant radically cutting wage bills by outsourcing production processes to wherever in the world could provide a good cheapest and to the required quality – which more often than not meant Asia.

So while the total number of Americans employed in the manufacturing industry fell from 20 million in 1980 to 17 million by 1990, China's manufacturing workforce rose from 59 million to 86 million during the same period.[24]

The Thatcher and Reagan policy revolution also freed company management to meet the growing consumer demand for more choice by establishing far more flexible and speedy production processes without fear of trade union opposition. New computing technologies and then the internet became vital, first to co-ordinating complex global production networks, then speeding up processes of design and manufacture and ultimately giving the customer much more direct say over the nature of the product. Without the political shifts launched by the New Right these changes would have been far slower and may well not have happened at all.

Highly regulated markets such as the financial sector could not have created the high speed, global approach to investment that was vital for firms outsourcing their production processes across the world. The emphasis on offering a wider range of products from a variety of different companies to meet consumer demand for choice and self-expression would not have happened if key economic sectors had remained as publicly owned monopolies. And the unions, whose power was extensive in the US and UK in the postwar period, would have used that power, had it not been destroyed, to resist company man-

---

24   US Bureau of Labor Statistics and Judith Banister, *Manufacturing Employment in China*: http://1.usa.gov/1UeWgDj

agement moves to restructure firms on a global basis and to outsource production to Asia.

Equally important though was the way Reagan and Thatcher set a tone for their own countries and ultimately the wider world. Their election and re-election in landslide victories, their radical policies and the fact that both the UK and US economies were booming by the late 1980s meant that their Hayekian message of an individualism released from the shackles of the big state and flourishing in the free market grew in credibility and influence. The collective, deferential values of the Big Power Consensus, already under assault following the 1960s social revolution, declined even further. Nowhere was this more apparent than in the collapsing membership of trade unions, which fell from 20% of the whole workforce in the early 1980s to just around 11% today in America.[25] In the UK, membership fell from a peak of 12 million in the late 1970s to 6.5 million today.[26]

The New Right revolution was far from being an unqualified victory for small power. One fundamental problem was the way the policies of Reagan and Thatcher weakened the power of the big state only to replace it with the power of big business and concentrated wealth. But the long-term result has also been a world where individual enterprise is more valued and where there is the necessary freedom in labour and company law to allow individuals to launch and operate businesses. It is also a world where the technology that enables entrepreneurialisation has been able to develop unimpeded.

---

25   US Bureau of Labor Statistics

26   Department for Business, Innovation and Skills, Trade Union Membership 2014, Statistical Bulletin

TECHNOLOGY DOESN'T CHANGE PEOPLE, PEOPLE DO

However, entrepreneurialisation is very far from being about the power of technology or politics alone. In fact, something far more profound is behind the trend – a revival of that small power spirit of freedom, choice and rebellion that inspired radicals like James Madison and Mary Wollstonecraft.

Personal computing and then the internet did not develop in a vacuum hermetically sealed from what was happening in wider society and politics. In both areas, technology has been influenced by the widespread shift towards small power values.

No one has done more to chart this shift than Ronald Inglehart from the University of Michigan. Inglehart suspected in the early 1970s that Western societies were moving from populations shaped by materialist values to post-materialist values or what his protégé Christian Welzel calls "emancipatory values". The first leads people to give utmost priority to earning a living, ensuring they and their families have enough to eat and securing decent housing. The latter means populations focus heavily on a search for autonomy, self-expression and personal fulfilment.

Inglehart's early surveys of Western populations showed clearly that older generations were much more likely to display materialist values, while emancipatory values strengthened among the younger generations. Inglehart faced a problem though. How could he prove that it wasn't just that as people got older they grew more materialistic? Maybe the idealism of youth fades as we take on the house and kids and we realise that actually being free to dance and paint is not really a great substitute for having some money in the bank. The only fool-proof solution was time.

Inglehart has now spent four decades surveying hundreds of

thousands of people's values and has built one of the most extensive and respected databases of global attitudes as a result. It is now beyond doubt that what Ronald Inglehart discovered in those early studies was something much more profound than age hardening our hearts. He had discovered a deep cultural shift.

Those younger generations in the early studies did not ditch emancipatory values as they grew older. In fact, they stayed remarkably committed to them, as have the subjects of the research born since then. So as older materialist generations have died out, the populations of the advanced economies have become far more focused on autonomy and self-expression than was the case throughout most of the 20th century and probably for centuries beforehand.

The result is a world where millions are much more inclined to adopt and adapt a technology that gives them greater capacity to fulfil their desire for autonomy and self-expression. The population of the 1940s was still reliant on routine jobs in large-scale industry. They were in thrall to the standardised products of that industry and constrained by strictly enforced social rules. And as Inglehart discovered, that generation were concerned mostly with survival and earning a living. Even if the internet had existed in the postwar era, people at that time simply did not have the desire to make use of the internet in the way it has been exploited by millions over the last 20 years. It is impossible, for example, to imagine the strait-laced, deferential generation of the 1940s and 1950s taking to YouTube to share their latest self-penned song, their deepest thoughts on their mental illness or their customisation of any manner of product from a film clip to a complex piece of games software.

The entrepreneurialisation of society of the last 40 years is, therefore, about far more than changing technologies or politics. It is driven by an intensification of that deep human desire for self-expression and self-determination that first sparked that rebellion against big power in the 1520s. The work of Ronald Inglehart and his associates has shown that what lies behind the recent upsurge in a small power economy are deep shifts in the way millions of people choose to live their lives and the aspirations they have for the future.

Our lives as consumers, and increasingly as workers, have taken a radical shift away from the hierarchical, centralised, bureaucratic model. The tools for creativity and innovation are now becoming so widespread and increasingly sophisticated that the distinction between consumer and producer is collapsing, and entrepreneurial skills, once assumed to belong only to an elite of risk-taking, highly innovative individuals, are now spreading throughout the population.

However, this small revolution is far from complete. A big obstacle stands in the way of further progress to a world where individual freedom, initiative and choice – and the huge diversity that results from that – flourish. That obstacle is big economic power.

13

A Not So Golden Isle

Something rather helpful happened to Gerald's family one thousand years ago. In 1066, a force led by William, Duke of Normandy, conquered England. The English monarch Harold was killed in battle and the Duke crowned himself King. William rapidly set about confiscating land from the English nobility and parcelling vast swathes of it out among his loyal supporters. One of those was Geoffrey De Mandeville who became one of the biggest landowners in the country, with an estate stretching across much of South East England. Another was Hugh D'Avranches, who was gifted vast stretches of the County of Cheshire in the Northwest.

As a devout Christian, De Mandeville gave a part of his estate to the Church, including a swathe of farmland and open fields called the Hundred Acres near the town of Westminster. This is where the Hundred Acres stayed for the next 400 years until King Henry VIII broke with the Catholic Church at the time of the Reformation and seized lands owned by English monasteries.

The land remained a possession of the monarchy for almost a century, until it was sold off by James I in 1623, and ended up ultimately in the hands of a moneylender, Alexander Davies. But Davies died at 29 in the outbreak of bubonic plague that swept across England in 1665. He left only one heir – a six-month old daughter called Mary.

Since a woman, let alone a young girl, could not be expected to own an estate in her own right, Mary was married at the age of 12 to the Earl of Chester, who happened to be a descendant of Hugh D'Avranches. So 600 years after King William I confiscated English land and handed it out among his favourites, the estates of Cheshire in the Northwest and the Hundred Acres were united in one family.

Chester was obviously a wealthy and powerful noble given his ownership of much of Cheshire. However, it was the inheritance of his very young wife which was to prove his descendants' fortune, for the Hundred Acres included areas that were to become known as Mayfair, Chelsea and London's West End – the most desirable and expensive residential and shopping districts in the UK, and arguably, the world.

As chance would have it, the Earl of Chester was Gerald's great, great, great, great, great, great grandfather. As a result, Gerald is now the richest person born in the UK with an estimated worth of around £8 billion. He is much better known by his title of the Duke of Westminster.

Take your pick of the fortuitous historical events that allowed the Duke to become so rich and powerful. Maybe it was the way Luther and Zwingli's revolution gave Henry VIII the pretext to enrich himself at the expense of the Church. Maybe it was the bubonic plague, which forced a 12-year-old girl to marry a powerful aristocrat. Most probably though, it was the fact that William, Duke of Normandy's military strategy proved successful against King Harold's army in 1066, allowing him to parcel out English land to his relatives and supporters. It was that 1,000-year-old event that was ultimately the source of Gerald Grosvenor's wealth in both Cheshire and London.

The Duke of Westminster is an example of a world that is still dominated by great concentrations of wealth. He is also a symbol of how that wealth ensures generations of the same family can stay at the top of the economic and social tree for centuries. In short, big economic power is incredibly resilient, despite everything the champions of small power have thrown at it over the last 500 years. He may be an extreme case, but he is far from unique.

GOLDEN ISLE

Let's imagine an island. It's an odd place. It only has a population of around 3,500 split up into 1,000 families or households. It doesn't own a lot – only £1 million between everyone. That amount takes the form of gold jewellery, which is highly prized by the islanders. Gold is very rare on the island – the jewellery is highly elaborate and very much in demand because how much someone owns has a huge impact on where they live, what they earn and the course of their life.

If wealth was distributed completely evenly on the island, every household would own £1,000 worth of jewellery. In fact, the distribution is nothing like that. The 1,000 families are split up into 10 villages of 100. The poorer you are the more easterly the village in which you live, battered by high winds and seared by burning sun. The better off you are, the more westerly your home, in the cool, calm shade of the island's mountains and forests. The most easterly five villages only have £100,000 worth of gold trinkets to go round, meaning on average, they each own jewellery with a value of £200.

But that £200 is just an average number. The poorest village of 100 families actually owns no jewellery, except maybe the odd bracelet or ring worth a few pounds. Each family in the next village along owns jewellery worth around £100 each – 10 times less than they would own under a completely equal distribution.

As we move west, each village owns larger, albeit still modest, amounts than the last until you get to the best off of the easterners – they own gold to the value of £500 each. Still only half what they would own under an equal distribution but very well-off compared to the most easterly village. Even though there is only 10% of that £1 million of property to go round those 500 families in the five eastern villages, it is still shared out very unequally. That leaves a whopping £900,000 worth of jewellery to be split among the five western villages.

Just like the poorest five villages, each western village owns more than the last as we move west. It's the villagers enjoying the cool breeze of the island's most westerly point who have really hit the ownership jackpot. They own £440,000 of the island's £1 million worth of jewellery. That's two-and-a-half times more than the neighbouring village and 44 times what the second most easterly village owns. In other words, the richest 10% of families own 44% of all the jewellery on the island. In fact, they own more golden jewellery than is owned by eight out of the ten villages together.

However, this masks a more significant concentration of wealth because the jewellery is not shared out equally, even within the wealthiest village. In fact, at the most westerly point of this most westerly village are the 10 wealthiest families on the island. They have £100,000 worth of jewellery to them-selves, giving them £10,000 each.

So on this strange island, the richest 10 families own as much jewellery as five easterly villages containing 500 families. This even makes this grouplet well-off compared to their nearest neighbours in the village, as the average wealth for that group of 100 is "only" £4,400. What does this mean for Golden Isle?

Fundamentally, it means that the richest 10 families just keep getting richer. Jewellery is valuable on the island because it is in demand. That means the richest can play the market much more effectively than anyone else. They can sell the jewels they own that are most desired, and thus the most expensive, and buy them back when they fall in price and sell others among their stash that have gone up in value.

But the big money comes from renting out their jewels to other people on the island who want to pretend how wealthy and tasteful they are even though they may in reality be an easterner. This is a thriving trade particularly because there are so few jewels to go round the rest of the population given the amount owned by the most westerly village. This costs the wealthiest practically nothing – they don't take the risk of selling anything at too low a price or losing their prized assets, they just earn money over and over again from what they already own.

It's a great way to make a living, especially given that many in the west inherited all the jewellery from their parents, who inherited it from theirs and so on. In fact, no less than one-third of all the jewellery on the island has been inherited from older family members.

For the rest of the inhabitants of Golden Isle there are far fewer opportunities to make money by buying and selling or renting out their assets. Instead, they have to work for a living, growing and cooking food, building and maintaining houses and, of course, fashioning and refashioning the jewellery for westerly villages.

Of course, Golden Isle has a very simple economy and a tiny population, but the way wealth is distributed is not really that unusual. In fact, it is identical to the way it is distributed in the UK with each village representing 10% of the UK population ordered according to their wealth. British people obviously hold that wealth in a variety of ways other than just as jewellery: pensions, cash, real estate, company shares and intellectual property. However, despite such economic complexity and sophistication, the wealthiest 10% really do own considerably more than 80% of the population, and the richest 1% has assets equivalent to the poorest 50%.[27]

Nor is Golden Isle very different to the rest of the world. Compare a range of advanced economies according to the way wealth is distributed and most have a very similar distribution of wealth. Golden Isle would, like the UK, if anything, be one of the more equal countries.

However, the concentration of economic power on Golden Isle and in the UK is nothing compared to the planet as a whole. According to a well-regarded analysis from the bank Credit Suisse, 50% of the world's population owns less than 1% of global wealth, while the wealthiest 10% own 87% and the wealthiest 1% own 48%.[28]

Imagine a different version of Golden Isle, where one village of families owns £870,000 worth of the jewellery, leaving just £130,000 to be shared out among the other 900. That is precisely how the world looks today. Wealth, which Madison and the other proponents of small power understood well is just another name for economic power and the political and cultural influence that comes with it, remains highly concentrated within a few hands.

THE BIG FOUR

However, levels of personal or household wealth only tell one

---

27   All data on UK distribution of wealth used here can be found at https://www.equality-trust.org.uk/

28   Credit Suisse *Global Wealth Report 2015:* http://bit.ly/1QmzRCB

side of the story of the concentration of economic power. The advocates of small power throughout the centuries have also been opponents of the way single organisations or a small number of organisations can exert control over large sections of the economy.

Indeed, Gerald Grosvenor may be rich beyond most people's wildest dreams by virtue of a 1,000-year-old inheritance, but it is nothing compared to those who exert monopoly power.

Carlos Slim is the CEO and Chairman of America Movil, which controls three-quarters of the fixed, mobile and broadband communications in Mexico. As the OECD found, this monopolistic position has not only made Slim absurdly wealthy – he has a personal wealth of $70 billion – it has, according to the OECD, also damaged innovation in the vital telecoms sector for Mexico, led to unfair prices for consumers and thus contributed overall to wider damage to Mexico's economy and levels of inequality, which are very high relative to other economies.

Slim and America Movil may represent a clear case of monopolistic control, but it is not rare to find oligopolistic control – where a handful rather than a single company controls a sector – in most advanced economies.

Many are aware of the phrase "too big to fail". It's another way of saying that too few banks control too much of the finance market to avoid vast government bailouts when they lose the confidence of their investors and customers. Even though the phrase became commonplace after the 2008 crash, little has changed in the world of finance.

Just five banks control almost half of banking assets in the biggest national economy in the world – the US. Just four banks hold three-quarters of the UK's 65 million personal current accounts and no less than 85% of all business current accounts. As a result, they are, unsurprisingly, also responsible for 90% of business loans.[29] But the UK and the US are not alone. In fact, the phrase "the Big Four" or "Big Five", used in the UK and the US to refer to the dominant banks, is also used in economies as diverse as Australia, China, Sweden and South Africa.

This tendency to concentrate power in the hands of four or five firms is not reserved to the banking sector. One study of the American economy found that in 2007 almost 40% of all the country's manufacturing sectors had four or fewer firms in control of 50% of that sector's business. In the UK, the top five firms in sectors as diverse as mobile phones, video games, fixed line telephony, air travel, cinemas and gas supply had a market share of over 75%.[30]

One result of this is that the top 200 US corporations accounted for no less than 30% of all business revenues in the US before the crash. It is worth reflecting on that – just 200 corporations controlling around one-third of an economy in which 30 million businesses operate. Globally, the situation is even starker with just 500 firms earning over a third of the world's business revenues before the crash.[31]

This has made some individual firms very well-known and very powerful. Walmart sells 57% of America's groceries. Between them, Amazon and Barnes and Noble account for 43% of all book sales. Miller-Coors and Anheuser sell an astounding 65% of all beer in the US. And just one company, Intel, controls 85% of the global market for microprocessors for personal computers.

A study in 2011 suggests that this global oligopoly is even more concentrated than it might at first appear. Using mathe-

---

29   According to the UK's Competition and Markets Authority: http://reut.rs/1Y0I86N

30   Maurice Saatchi, *The Road from Serfdom:* http://bit.ly/1Y0HZAd

31   John Bellamy Foster et al., *Monopoly and Competition in Twenty-First Century Capitalism:* http://bit.ly/1SgX3ZV/

matical modelling, the Swiss Federal Institute of Technology analysed the share ownerships of 43,000 global corporations. They found that just 1,318 firms effectively owned a wide range of other firms accounting for 80% of global business revenues. Going further, the analysts discovered that ownership of the 1,318 firms themselves resided with a particularly tight-knit group of companies numbering only 147, most of which were, of course, banks including Barclays, J.P. Morgan and Goldman Sachs.[32]

BIG GETS BIGGER

It is tempting to believe that there is something natural or inevitable about such high concentrations of economic power given the prevalence of oligopoly and the scale of household wealth inequality. Indeed, many economists have argued that market economies work most efficiently when the incentives for the most successful and wealthy entrepreneurs are high and when competition exists between a handful of firms rather than many. This, however, overlooks the fact that the very high levels of concentrated economic power described here are very recent.

The number of American manufacturing industries controlled by four or fewer firms has risen enormously from around 12% of all sectors in the early 1970s to the 35% mentioned above in 2007. The revenue of the top 200 US corporations stood at 24% in the early 1970s before rising to 30% in 2008. The top 500 global corporations may earn a third of all business revenues now, but it was less than a fifth in the 1960s.[33]

---

32 *New Scientist,* "Revealed: The Capitalist Network that Runs the World"

33 John Bellamy Foster et al., *Monopoly and Competition in Twenty-First Century Capitalism:* http://bit.ly/1SgX3ZV

The share of total income earned by the top 1% of families in the USA now stands at 20% but 40 years ago it was 10%. The change in the share of wealth is even more striking with just 160,000 families or 0.1% of households now owning 22% of the value of all US assets up from just 7% in the early 1970s. By contrast, the wealth of 90% of US households has fallen from around 35% in the mid-1980s to 23% today.[34]

Similar trends are underway in the UK. The average income of someone in the richest 0.1% has risen from approximately £450,000 per year in the mid-1990s to £1,300,000 in 2010. The top 10% of male earners have seen their weekly earnings double from £500 per week in the early 1970s to over £1,000 by 2008 while the median has risen from £300 to just over £500 and the poorest have seen a rise from £200 to around £300.[35]

THE GREAT CONTRADICTION

It is clear from this data that economic power is not only highly concentrated but is becoming more so. Over the last 30 years a smaller number of individuals and their families have secured control of a larger proportion of assets and the revenues associated with them. Alongside this, smaller numbers of companies have secured control of a growing number of markets.

A great deal has been written about the impact of such concentration of economic power and the linked issue of inequality. Detailed analysis shows how concentrated economies perform worse on a wide range of measures from health and educational outcomes, to levels of crime, to innovation and growth.

---

34 Data can be found at www.inequality.org
35 Data can be found at https://www.equalitytrust.org.uk/

However, what many have failed to notice is the emergence of a central contradiction. We now live in an economic world characterised by a small power spirit. Consumers are gaining greater and greater control over the nature of the products and services they purchase to the point where the line between producer and consumer is disappearing. Workers seek out greater autonomy and creativity with many now taking the plunge into self-employment to free them from the dominance of the corporate structure. New technologies, such as blockchain, will enable an ever greater deepening of this small revolution.

This is, in short, a long backlash against the dominance and concentration of economic power in large corporations during the 20th century. It is a trend intimately linked to the same spirit forging small revolutions against concentrated big power also occurring in the political and cultural spheres. All of this is driven by the hugely significant shift in values identified by Inglehart.

However, just as the tools and the desire for greater economic autonomy, choice and creativity are spreading, the underlying ownership of the resources which can enable the use of those tools and the fulfilment of that desire is becoming more concentrated in fewer hands. If we are drifting back to a world of concentrated economic power where assets and revenues accrue largely to those that are already wealthy or to organisations that already control markets, then we will not only turn back the clock on a period of enormous human advance, we will also squander the great opportunity presented by an era where more people than ever are looking to exercise the self-determination, creativity and wealth creation of the entrepreneur.

BIG ECONOMIC POWER: KEEPING YOU DOWN

We can see this problem most clearly when we look at the link between high levels of concentrated economic power and the likelihood of people within a population to move up or down the income and wealth scale. Or to extend the Golden Isle metaphor, moving from one village to another. What sociologists and economists call "social mobility".

The evidence that more unequal economies also tend to be less socially mobile is now very strong. A Canadian economics professor, Miles Corak, published what he called The Great Gatsby Curve in 2012 reproduced below. This mapped the extent to which different generations of the same family had different levels of income (or what Corak calls "intergenerational earnings elasticity") for a wide variety of countries against the levels of inequality in those countries. What he found is incontrovertible: nations with higher levels of inequality are very likely to have lower levels of social mobility.

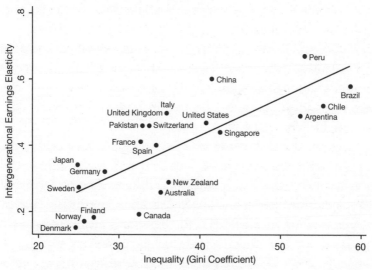

Source: Miles Corak (2012), available at milescorak.com

This suggests very strongly that as smaller numbers of individuals and organisations gain control of assets, revenues and markets, the likelihood that they will retain that control grows. Hence that hugely important link between economic reward and enterprise is broken. Instead, wealth simply accrues to those who already hold it. You can be as enterprising and as creative as you want but your chances of receiving an economic benefit in return are actually shrinking as economic power becomes more concentrated. In fact, the best way to become wealthy is to be wealthy already and use your assets to generate income by playing the markets and renting out your possessions just as the most westerly 10 families do on Golden Isle.

There is clearly an issue of straightforward justice in all this – why should the well-off and powerful get better off and more powerful just because they already are or because they inherited such wealth and power from their parents? This offends the very values that we now widely accept following the moral defeat of feudalism and absolute monarchy. But it also raises two big questions about our future.

First, the divorce of wealth and power from birth and position was far from perfect in the 18th and 19th centuries, but it did occur enough to generate the huge human advances of Deirdre McCloskey's Great Fact. If that link is being reinstated if not wholly but in some part, then we risk slower economic growth, innovation and advances in human well-being than we might otherwise enjoy as a result.

Second, the rise of the small power spirit means that the opportunity exists to exceed even that which was achieved in the last 250 years. That progress was the achievement largely of elite groups of entrepreneurs and technical specialists such as engineers and scientists. But the emerging small power revolution of the last 30 years holds out the possibility that much, much larger numbers are willing and able to be entrepreneurial and creative. It is possible that with far greater numbers engaged in wealth creation and innovation than ever before, living standards, public benefit and human well-being could make ever greater leaps forward. But this will only happen if those entrepreneurial and creative behaviours are adequately rewarded and respected.

The evidence already exists showing the importance of this link between a future of innovation and progress and breaking down big economic power. The Global Creativity Index is a study of innovation across the nations of the world led by Professor Richard Florida and produced by the Martin Prosperity Institute at the University of Toronto. It ranks countries according to three measures:

- technology: the amount a nation spends on and allocates human resources to research and development as well as its patented innovations

- talent: the educational attainment of a nation's population and the percentage of its workforce committed to creative professions

- tolerance: the extent to which a nation is open to new ideas and different lifestyles measured as openness to people of different ethnicity and sexuality.

Measuring these characteristics against an economy's levels of inequality, it found that while tolerance was not clearly related to concentrated economic power, talent and technology most definitely were. In other words, the more unequal an economy the less likely it was to be oriented towards innovation or to have a workforce engaged in creative activities. As the survey's authors themselves said:

We find that the Global Creativity Index is in fact systematically associated with lower levels of socio-economic inequality—and hence greater equality—across the nations of the world . . . We believe (this) overall finding . . . to be an important one, for it implies that the general trajectory of economic development is associated with lower levels of inequality.

The study does seem to suggest that there can be a fair bit of variation in levels of inequality among highly creative nations. Sweden (a relatively more equal nation) takes the top spot but the US (far less equal) is in second place. However, the overall pattern is clear that higher levels of equality and creativity go hand in hand. It is particularly striking that four small countries in one region of Europe, and which have a strong history of valuing economic equality, all appear in the top 10 of the Global Creativity Index: Sweden, Finland, Norway and Denmark.

So we are at a historical turning point. One where the growing concentration of economic power slows the advances made in recent centuries or one where the clear link between innovative enterprise and economic reward drives forward a new era of mass creativity and human progress. Our choice is the stifling structures of big economic power or the liberating creativity of small, distributed power. The question now is how we secure the latter.

14

Unleashing Small Economic Power

THE WRONG TURN OF STATE SOCIALISM

The solution developed by 20th century socialism for addressing inequality was the big state. By the 1940s the left was wholly committed to the idea that governments had to actively correct the inequality inherent in the free market by taxing the wealthy more heavily and redistributing the revenues to the less well-off. The redistribution took the form either of direct cash transfers (as pensions or social security payments) or the establishment of large-scale public services, most notably healthcare and education systems.

This was also a period when the left (and an increasing number on the right) believed governments could use their power to plan and regulate economies to limit unemployment, maintain high pay and prevent the economic volatility that led to poverty and higher levels of inequality. To this end some socialist states actually took over the running of large sections of the economy, particularly in key sectors such as transport, communications and energy.

It is probably fair to say that very many on the left of politics still look back to the postwar era of the big state with fondness. Particularly since the 2008 crash, there has been a

179

new confidence on the left for demands such as much tougher regulation by governments of pay and employment, higher taxes to support expanded public services and even some calls for a new wave of public ownership. There has also been a vigorous defence of the established welfare state in the face of government cuts following the higher levels of public borrowing and lower tax revenues caused by the crash and ensuing recession.

In effect, the left's solution to high concentrations of economic power within corporations and wealthy households is to establish a countervailing concentration of economic power within the state, which will, in theory, use that power on behalf of the less well-off.

For those who care about small power this is not an adequate solution. The small power vision that had its origins in the values of the Reformation period and which was transformed into a more general programme by American revolutionaries and European Radicals was designed to dissolve *all* forms of concentrated power: economic, social *and* political. Small power historically was opposed to the superrich, the clergy *and* the dictator. Their vision was of a world where individuals were free enough and wealthy enough to make entirely autonomous decisions about their own lives without seeking the permission or support of anyone else. As we saw, this spirit played a big part in shaping the outlook of many socialists well into the early 20th century.

It was only with the rise of the Big Power Consensus that socialism rejected its old small power roots and placed its faith in the power of big government to bring about a more equal society. This was and remains a highly problematic approach for three reasons.

FREEDOM VERSUS EQUALITY

Most importantly, it sets equality against freedom. Sometimes implicitly but often explicitly, socialists believe that the only way to deliver a more equal economy is to curtail the free choice of individuals. This obviously reached its most absurd and inhumane form in the communist systems of the Soviet Union and China and their various imitators across the globe in the last century. But the sentiment is also there, albeit in a far less malign form, in democratic socialism. The secret to addressing inequality is to use the unique power of the state to coerce people to do things they might otherwise not do: pay higher taxes, respect state-sanctioned monopolies, abide by regulatory controls on market activity. Failure to do so will lead to prosecution by a state backed up by the power of an organised police force and, in extreme circumstances, the army.

Socialists may not like to acknowledge it but these are all practices that have their historical origin in the absolutist states of the 18th century. Louis XIV and his administrators may have developed and refined the techniques of central state control with an eye on security, order and personal power rather than economic equality, but the opposition to the theory and practice of individual freedom and distributed, small power was clear.

Those who valued *both* freedom *and* equality saw the powerful central state as an enemy, not as an ally. American revolutionaries, European Radicals and early socialists recognised that fair shares of wealth owned and controlled by individuals, their families and their communities was the route to a society made up of citizens free and resourced to make their own choices in life. Twentieth century socialists forgot this tradition when they fell in love with the power of the state. Instead of finding ways to spread the individual ownership of wealth as a route to equality and freedom, they vested wealth in the state or simply taxed the wealthy and made citizens, particularly the poorest, dependent on the state as a source of income, education and healthcare. It was an enormous, historical wrong turn that betrayed the genuine radicalism of small power.

THE ROBIN HOOD PARADOX

Their adoration of big governmental power also meant that 20th century socialism overstated the significance of the state as a source of greater equality. Peter Lindert is a distinguished professor of economics at the University of California. He has spent much of his career understanding the impact of public spending on society and, in particular, taking a very long historical view. His studies prompted him to develop one of the most important but maybe also most neglected ideas in public policy: the Robin Hood Paradox.

Lindert argues that a wide range of research has identified six main elements that can affect whether an economy moves towards greater economic equality or inequality at any particular time. They are:

- population growth

- the rate at which the skills of the workforce improve

- technological change

- shifts in demand for certain products

- the influence of labour market organisations such as unions

- redistribution by the state.

Following his own study of 20th century history and an extensive survey of other research, Lindert concludes that the trend towards greater economic equality between the 1920s and 1970s in the US and the UK, and then a contrasting trend thereafter, is largely the result of the first five factors. The impact of state redistribution, he admits, is difficult to quantify but is very likely to have only played a small part for three reasons.

First, a great part of the earlier trend to equality and then to inequality later in the 20th century resulted from changes in the gap between those on higher and lower incomes. This could not have been the result of tax and spend policies, which only kick in after income levels have been decided by employers. Second, the changes in incomes occurred across a wide range of nations, which had very different approaches to the degree of state redistribution. And third, the decline in the incomes of the richest in the early 20th century began to occur well before the state began significantly ramping up taxes in the late 1930s.

In fact, Lindert comes to an even more striking conclusion. Historically, higher levels of state redistribution have only occurred in periods when the five other factors have already delivered a great economic levelling. At times when those factors are promoting inequality, the state actually becomes less redistributive. He calls this the Robin Hood Paradox, for as he explains: "Robin Hood's redistributive army is missing when and where it is most needed."

We can speculate at length, and some have, about why such a counter-intuitive paradox exists, but the important point to note here is that it utterly contradicts the story that state socialism tells about itself: that parties of the left secure power to right the great injustice of deeply unequal economies. In fact, they are far better seen as the Jonny-come-latelies of egalitarianism, pronouncing themselves the saviours of humanity when a great deal of the salvation has already been achieved.

The Paradox also raises a major and maybe insuperable political challenge for the traditional left. If they cannot secure the necessary power to create a more equal society precisely at the time when an economy is moving towards greater inequality, then what exactly is the point of state socialism? There is something deeply flawed about a strategy if it only becomes operational when it is least needed and fails to deliver when it is most required.

THE SCULLY LIMIT

The socialist focus on the state is also challenged by another strand of often overlooked economic research – that of Gerald Scully and Liveo Di Matteo. Scully was best known as one of the first people to study the economics of the sports industry, but he also explored the relationship between the size of government and economic growth. By studying a range of different tax arrangements across US states he concluded that up to a certain point, the increasing size of government helps generate higher levels of economic growth, but beyond that point the benefits begin to trail off and ultimately begin to actually prevent growth. In his 1994 paper, he estimated that the optimum point for the size of the state with regards to generating economic growth was around 20% of the size of the overall economy.

Inspired by Scully's approach, the Canadian economist Liveo Di Matteo updated and expanded his method in 2013 by studying the link between government size and growth across 186 countries. He found an identical effect to Scully, albeit with a higher optimal state size of 30% of the overall economy.

More directly relevant from our perspective, however, is that Di Matteo went one step further than Scully and explored whether there was also an optimum size for the state with regards to delivering social outcomes such as better health, educational achievement, life satisfaction and living standards.

What he found is telling. The social benefits of a bigger state rise significantly particularly when public spending grows from 20% of the whole economy to 35%. But once the state expands beyond that size, the social impact of greater spending has far less positive impact on health, education and the other benefits we may wish to achieve. That finding also needs to be set against the fact that while an expanding state beyond 35% of the whole economy may deliver some social benefits, it is also likely to be slowing economic growth, which will have its own negative social impact.

Going into more detail, Di Matteo also found that the benefits of health and education spending were great when those priorities rose from 20% to 25% of total public spending, (rather than of the whole economy) but once they got much bigger than this the benefits trailed off rapidly. Interestingly, he also discovered that states could achieve similar levels of outcomes whether social protection took up a relatively large or relatively small share of total spending, suggesting that the way welfare systems are designed, rather than their size, is crucial to determining their benefit to society.

These findings are once again extremely challenging for those who see the state as the best route to a more equal and fairer economy. The left has traditionally opposed any significant reductions in the size of the state and regularly lobbies for an ever bigger share of public spending to go towards health, education and welfare priorities. Indeed, most socialists in Europe are currently engaged in a fierce political battle over austerity policies. Their aim is to protect states which operate with spending levels of 45% to 50% of the overall economy rather than closer to the 30% to 35% that Scully and Di

Matteo's work suggests is optimum for a combination of high economic growth and impactful social outcomes.

Finally, it is vital to acknowledge that state socialism was very much a creature of a particular era – the Big Power Consensus of the 20th century. As we have seen there was widespread faith at that time from all economic classes, political viewpoints and intellectuals in the capacity of concentrated economic, social and political power to achieve all manner of beneficial outcomes. That era is well and truly over. The cultural shifts since the 1960s combined with the massive technological change that began in the 1970s mean that we now live in a world shaped by a much greater desire for self-determination free of the constraints imposed by large, hierarchical, centralised and bureaucratic institutions in both the private and public sector.

These are profound changes that cannot be wished away. In fact, as Ronald Inglehart's and Christian Welzel's work showed, they only seem to be getting stronger. Under such conditions we need a completely different approach to creating a more equal economy, one that respects the small power goals of free choice, self-determination and well-resourced and well-rewarded individual enterprise.

As the work of Miles Corak and the team behind the Global Creativity Index revealed, high concentrations of economic power break the link between reward and enterprise, leading to less innovative, creative economies. The solution, however, cannot be to simply concentrate economic power elsewhere.

This does not mean there is no role for the state but it *is* a radically different one from that envisioned by the big power left. Rather than being about a day-to-day management of redistributive mechanisms and public services, the state should instead focus on changing the rules by which economic activity is undertaken so that it generates a more distributed allocation of resource and reward. At its most fundamental this means reforming how assets and the returns they generate are shared out so that they are less concentrated in the hands of a relatively small group of individual households and corporations.

In particular, the state needs to revise the laws and practices around ownership of assets and wealth, rather than focusing almost entirely on trying to equalise incomes. Only with such a focus can we create that more egalitarian but free economy that people like James Madison and Mary Wollstonecraft envisaged.

REDEFINING OWNERSHIP

The starting point must be to rethink the structures of the corporation. Currently, there is a dominant model of corporate ownership that was developed in the 19th and 20th centuries as part of the rise of the Big Power Consensus. There are effectively three partners in this structure, each of whom has a different claim on the wealth and revenues generated by the corporation.

- The legal owners of the company who have the right to use and dispose of the assets of the firm as they see fit. Importantly they also have the right to use the firm's profits as they wish within the bounds of the law. Of course as successful firms grow those assets and the profits they generate can be extremely substantial.

- The employees of a company have no right to assets or profits but do have the right to a wage in return for their labour, which is drawn from the revenues of the firm.

- Finally there is the consumer, who has the right to a product or service in return for payment.

This is now such a well-established and widely employed model that it is largely taken for granted. But it represents one underlying reason why economic power and wealth is now so concentrated. By restricting the right to use and dispose of a firm's assets to the relatively small group of a firm's legally recognised owners, wealth, or more precisely the control of that wealth, is inevitably concentrated in only a few hands.

As the economic historian and statistician, Thomas Piketty has shown in *Capital in the 21st Century*, this structure ensures increasing concentration of economic power over time as the return on investment (the profits and the rise in value of assets secured by owners) tends to grow faster than any rise in wages.

From the point of view of just returns, it is also not entirely clear why such a model should exist at all. The owners of a company, who may be its founders, but also its investors in the form of shareholders, are vital to a firm's existence and success, however, the current structure rather assumes that they are infinitely more important than any other group. It is an approach that overlooks the fact that employees also play an absolutely fundamental role in the creation of profits and the growth in the value of a company's assets. Why this is ignored when considering who has a legal claim on assets or profits is far from obvious from a moral standpoint.

There is also the shifting role of the consumer to consider. As consumers become far more actively engaged in the research, design and development of services and products, they take on a role far closer to that of the employee. Increasingly, it is the ideas, insights and activities of consumers that shape a successful company. Companies like Lego and Procter & Gamble have become hugely successful by engaging customers directly in the development of products. Newer firms like

Facebook, Twitter and YouTube are little more than platforms for their consumers to develop content for sharing. This is the fundamental offer that creates growth in asset value and profits for those firms. Indeed, it is the network of consumers and their active engagement that is the prime asset of such firms. If we are to address the concentration of economic power and create instead an economy where enterprise and innovation rather than position and power is rewarded, this structure needs to be radically changed.

Governments should establish long-term programmes to weaken the grip of the established shareholder model and instead encourage the growth of so-called "mutual" models that provide both employees and consumers with ownership rights over assets and profits alongside a firm's directors and investors. It is not for the state to determine what those models should be, but a range of alternatives should be provided with significant tax advantages over the conventional structure. Indeed, such schemes do already exist but they should play a far more central and ambitious role in promoting alternative ownership models. For example, the schemes that currently exist in the UK provide tax advantages to the employees who take part in relatively modest share ownership schemes. By contrast, governments should explore how firms themselves could be incentivised to embrace mutual structures by providing tax breaks on profits and increases in the value of assets.

Government could themselves create new influential corporate models by restructuring firms they currently own in sectors such as energy, transport and, more recently banking, as employee and customer owned bodies. Currently, most privatisations repeat the mistakes of the sell-offs of the 1980s and 1990s, which simply transfer ownership of companies from the hands of the big state to the hands of the big investors, doing nothing meaningful to challenge concentrations of economic power.

Trade unions also have an important role to play. Unions are currently a relic of the Big Power Consensus, focused almost entirely on demanding higher incomes for workers within large corporations and defending a top-down, 20th century approach to welfare and public services. As a result, they have become tired, declining and increasingly ineffective institutions.

Refocusing themselves on a vision of creating a new and lasting settlement for employees and consumers that provides them with a fair share of wealth could refresh this outdated set of organisations. Unions could break with their main current activity – the endless cycle of annual wage deal negotiations – and instead become a real movement again, pressing firms to restructure themselves around mutual arrangements to give their employees and customers the rights to ownership they are due with all the financial benefits, such as shares of profits and asset appreciation that would follow.

REVIVING ANTITRUST

In the early 20th century there were vigorous popular demands in the US for laws to stop or reverse the rise of monopolistic and oligopolistic companies. Governments were forced to respond and a series of "antitrust" laws were passed which gave the state considerable powers to prevent market dominance by one or more firms.

Inspired by the vision of the founders of the American nation, antitrust law was enacted to prevent large corporations creating inequality in both the economic and political realm. As a result, governments and the courts applied the law very much in that spirit making antitrust a significant counter-vailing force to the rise of the big corporations.

However, that spirit declined in the 1980s. As president, Ronald Reagan appointed economists to positions of power in executive agencies and in the courts, who were convinced that antitrust policy needed to focus exclusively on economic efficiency. They were led by William F. Baxter whom Reagan appointed in his first year in office as head of antitrust enforcement. Over time this meant that courts and ultimately the Supreme Court shifted the focus of antitrust law away from considering the impact of corporate behaviour on economic and political equality, and almost entirely towards what was supposedly good for the consumer and the economy as a whole.

This inevitably meant a more permissive environment for mergers and acquisitions. As a result, another wave of those began in the 1980s. Despite this and the consequent rise in oligopolies detailed above, there are still some who argue for a further weakening of antitrust law by removing any concern for consumer welfare and focusing exclusively on what promotes economic growth and profitability regardless of any impact on the customer. Given that concern about the higher prices consumers might pay could be seen as the only aspect of antitrust law which now has some focus on equality, such a move would be extremely damaging from the perspective of achieving a small, distributed economy.

Rather than making such a counterproductive shift, antitrust law in the US as well as in other advanced economies and the European Union needs to embrace the spirit of the early 20th century by reacting against a new era of oligopoly just as the lawmakers of that period reacted against the merger mania of the 1890s.

Two law professors, Jonathan Baker and Steven Salop, recently considered how antitrust law might re-embrace this spirit. They made a number of suggestions including:

- Increasing budgets for antitrust agencies.

- Giving priority to antitrust cases in markets such as food, retail, energy and healthcare where uncompetitive practices have a bigger impact on middle-income and low-income earners, while giving a lesser priority to cases in markets focused on richer consumers.

- Requiring corporations involved in mergers or potentially uncompetitive practices to take action to limit the impact on less well-off customers; the authors cite the case of Comcast's acquisition of NBC-Universal, which was only allowed to go ahead on condition that broadband charges for poorer users was subsidised by the company.

- Taking a deliberately more aggressive and interventionist approach to antitrust in order to deter uncompetitive practices more widely.

- Adopting an approach enshrined in European Union law that allows companies to face antitrust action if they abuse their dominant market position no matter how they achieved that position. In the US, companies can only face prosecution if it can be shown that they deliberately excluded others from a market on their way to achieving market dominance. By contrast, the EU launched actions against two vast, high profile companies with very different routes to the top – Google and Gazprom – in 2015, on "abuse of dominant position" grounds.

But perhaps the most direct proposal made by the authors is simply to make preventing inequality a specific goal of antitrust law. If a company or group of companies was behaving in an anticompetitive way that increased the concentration of economic power and resources at the expense of the majority of citizens, they would be more likely to face prosecution, punishment and remedy.

Baker and Salop admit that such a provision would raise many challenging legal questions which would require resolution, but that is what courts are regularly required to do.

Strengthening and refocusing antitrust law and practice in this way would be an exceptionally powerful method to address the concentration of economic resources. It is also a perfect case of a small power solution. Although the state is using its coercive power in antitrust, it is doing it in a way that resets the underlying rules of the economy. Rather than intervening on a daily basis, the state is creating a more dynamic and competitive market economy and thus promoting liberty and equality simultaneously, rather than setting those ideals against each other by concentrating resources and power within the state itself.

HOMES FOR ALL

A vast part of a nation's wealth takes the form of real estate. In the US, around 30% of all households' wealth is their own home.[36] In the UK, 37% of the whole nation's wealth takes the form of real estate. So how this form of wealth is distributed will have a major impact on the concentration of economic power. Unsurprisingly, it is distributed very unequally.

All the houses in the UK together are worth around £3,500 billion. The wealthiest 10% own about £1,300 billion of this. The next wealthiest 10% own about £700 billion and the remaining 80% own £1,500 billion between them. In other

---

36   Data from the United States Census Bureau http://www.census.gov/people/wealth/

words the richest 20% own almost 60% of all the housing wealth in the UK.[37]

For the proponents of small power during the 18th and 19th centuries a reasonably fair division of land was a crucial feature of their vision of a society of independent, secure citizens. This was not just because land was the main productive asset of a time that was primarily agricultural but also because ownership of a piece of significant capital conferred economic security and a profound rootedness. Put most simply, it gave people a stake in society and their locality, thus transforming their relationship to that society, encouraging active citizenship and loyalty to their fellows.

The combination of owning capital in modern businesses and one's own home plays the same role today, giving people that dual stake in the economy and a locality that land once offered. As a result, surveys consistently show higher levels of life satisfaction and health among those who own their own homes. A recent study by the Royal Society of the Arts also showed that those who own their home are more likely to start their own business, helped, almost certainly, by the ability to use the house as collateral for business funding but also by the greater confidence and security home ownership confers.

It is no coincidence, therefore, that the spread of home ownership in the second half of the 20th century coincided with the emergence of the small revolution and the backlash against the Big Power Consensus. Owning your own home is one of the great overlooked causes of the rise in the postwar period of independent self-confidence and desire for personal liberty which underpinned the moves towards a smaller economy, politics and culture. The fact that home ownership is now in

---

37   Data from the UK's Office for National Statistics: http://bit.ly/24hLdix

decline in both the US[38] and the UK[39] is therefore an extremely detrimental trend, which must be rapidly reversed. Just as with the weakening of antitrust law, the decline of home ownership means we are at risk of losing the two major counter-trends that existed during the Big Power Consensus of the 20th century that ensured it was not as damaging as it might otherwise have been.

So, what is behind this negative housing trend? It begins with a failing market. A simple logic underpins properly functioning markets. As demand grows for a product, prices rise. As prices rise more producers rush in to create and sell the product to take advantage of those higher prices usually backed by return hungry investors. As a result, prices begin to drop as competition intensifies, productivity improves and more products flood the market. Over time this means that consumers not only get a better deal but also less well-off consumers are able to purchase the product. We see this happening over and over again most notably with new technology such as mobile phones, which were once the status symbol of the spendthrift city trader and now are an affordable and indispensable business tool for frugal Kenyan farmers (as well as everyone else).

Given the extraordinary prices that real estate can now secure in UK and US cities, and the millions desperate to find an affordable home, it is strange, to say the least, that the normal rules of a market do not operate. Surely, there should be millions of houses and apartments being built as developers seek to get in early and make a killing. If such a process was in operation, we would not only see many more dwellings being built, but owning your own home would be an affordable aspiration. Wealth would be distributed more widely in a way

---

38   A good summary of US home ownership data can be found at http://bit.ly/24hBo41
39   A good summary of UK home ownership data can be found at http://bit.ly/1t4PWYh

completely in line with small economic principles. The reason the market does not work in this way is for two reasons, both the result of undue concentrations of power.

First, there is the excessive control the state has over the permission to build. Both the UK and the US are tied up in complex planning and zoning regulations that make house-building expensive, time-consuming and uncertain. They also rule out obvious market-led responses to high demand such as building tall apartment blocks in central London. One survey of 100 housebuilding firms in the UK found that 80% cited planning restrictions as the factor having the most negative impact on their ability to build.[40]

Second, building requires space but it is exceptionally difficult to find and develop reasonably priced land. Instead of a transparent functioning market populated by a wide variety of competing sellers, the UK's land is owned by a tiny elite, most of whom, like Gerald Grosvenor, have inherited their highly lucrative possession. One assessment has concluded that just 0.6% of the British population own 69% of the nation's land.[41]

This means that land, much like the other sectors mentioned above, is in effect an oligopoly with the sellers having too much control to sell when they desire at any price that suits them. In fact, the market in land in the UK is so dysfunctional that there are no clear price signals at all. Instead, developers employ a formula called "residual land value" to work out what they should offer to landowners.[42]

One particularly pernicious practice is landbanking where owners lucky enough to hold space primed for development

40   Knight Frank *Building Momentum Housebuilding Report 2014*: http://bit.ly/1sYxylo

41   Kevin Cahill, *Who Owns Britain: the hidden facts behind landownership in the UK and Ireland*

42   Toby Lloyd, *Understanding and adapting the land market is key to solving our housing crisis*: http://bit.ly/22vrbSm

– sometimes even with permission to develop – simply hold the land while it rockets in price. It's a case of an overheated market desperate for supply being heated even further by the deliberate withholding of supply – a precise example of oligopolistic behaviour.

Clearly, breaking up the landowners' oligopoly would not only be an act akin to the antitrust programme outlined above, but it would also be a crucial building block in creating a more affordable housing market and hence widening the ownership of assets and wealth.

One country that is taking steps to do just this is Scotland, where it is estimated that just 432 people out of the population of five million own half the land.[43] There, the government is introducing a Land Reform Act which will give a new Land Reform Commission the power to take action against landowners who stand in the way of development, will introduce transparency into land ownership and the value of land, and will end the generous tax subsidies that bizarrely still exist for some of the wealthiest landowners.

Most interestingly, the money saved from ending these subsidies will be used to extend community buyouts of land to one million acres from the current 500,000 by 2020. These schemes, which bear a close resemblance to the business mutuals mentioned above, are based on a 2003 law that gives communities of residents and workers on a piece of land the right to buy it when it comes up for sale. It's an approach which could spread land ownership, and hence wealth more widely, but has also shown how it can bring long neglected tracts back into development, including for the building of homes.

---

43 The Final Report of the Land Reform Review Group: http://bit.ly/22vrn3Q

TAX SHIFT

Tax is a form of big power state coercion and not something that should be proposed lightly. One of the major errors of today's state socialists is their adherence to the idea that higher taxes are automatically good and act as the most powerful force for the promotion of a more equal economy. Nevertheless, the democratic state *can* be a profound force for good as long as it does not get too big as the work of Gerald Scully and Liveo Di Matteo has shown. If the optimal size of government spending is 30% to 35% of total economic output then this clearly requires significant taxation, although much lower than that currently operating in most western economies.

How that tax is raised can have a major impact on equality and concentration of economic power. Most advanced economies currently raise the bulk of their revenues by taxing wages through income taxes and taxing trade through sales and profit taxes. Assets and wealth in the form of property, land, capital gains, inheritance and large cash savings such as pensions pots tend to be subject to lower rates and even various forms of tax relief.

To be serious about rewarding and encouraging mass enterprise and innovation while addressing concentrations of economic power, this emphasis needs to shift. Those individuals, families and organisations with large wealth and assets should bear the greater burden of funding a small but socially impactful state, while middle and low earners should be resourced and rewarded as fully as possible without undue tax pressure.

The idea of taxing wealth more heavily has secured interest from policymakers around the world in recent years as growing levels of inequality have moved up the political agenda. Proposals are many, including, for example, raising existing taxes on wealth such as capital gains, introducing new taxes on high value houses and land or simply using a straightforward tax on anyone with wealth or assets over a certain level such as operates in France and Norway.

However, these proposals are often made without any commitment to reduce income, employment and trade taxes. They are simply proposed as a way to increase state revenues for goals such as reducing public debt or improving public services. Rather than increasing taxes, governments should introduce programmes to reduce the overall burden of tax by shrinking state spending while simultaneously shifting the focus of that tax burden.

It is notable, therefore, that President Obama committed himself in his State of the Union address in 2015 to a raft of wealth taxes – including higher capital gains and inheritance taxes and a fee on financial institutions with assets of over $50 billion – without actually increasing the overall tax take. Much of the extra revenue will be returned to middle earners through higher tax credits. Predictably, Republicans have reacted negatively to the proposals, seemingly unaware of how shifting taxation in this way is far truer to the vision of the founding fathers than their knee-jerk defence of a super-rich class and the big businesses they own.

A COMMUNITY FUND

A further method for distributing ownership and its proceeds more widely is the establishment of a community fund. The idea, first proposed by the economist James Meade, is relatively simple. The state, or some agency of the state, purchases shares in a nation's businesses and builds up a significant investment fund over time. The return generated for the fund is then distributed to a nation's citizens for their own purposes, rather than being used by shareholders for their own enrichment or investment elsewhere.

The US state of Alaska has run such a fund since 1976. Using revenues from the oil industry for long-term investment, it has grown from its initial size of $734,000 to over $40 billion today. The fund pays out an annual dividend to every long-term Alaskan resident, which has averaged $1,309 per year over the last 10 years.

James Meade placed such an idea at the heart of his vision for a "property owning democracy" built upon a more equal sharing of capital and wealth rather than the equalisation of income through tax and spend policies. He felt the community fund was such an important mechanism that he suggested it would aim, over time, to own 50% of national assets to ensure capital was shared out fairly.

The idea is attractive because it is clearly a way of challenging concentrations of economic power and distributing the proceeds of productive activity widely, rather than into the hands of a small minority. One of its great advantages is that it provides a lump sum to citizens, which could be used as capital by many for business and other creative activities. This makes it an apt response and probable accelerator for the entrepreneurialisation trends identified earlier.

The community fund's main weakness is that its existence is entirely reliant on the coercive power of the state to raise taxes or, on one proposal, demand shares to provide the fund with its investment capital. It also runs the risk of becoming, like so many state run investment vehicles, the preserve of officials operating in an opaque and undemocratic fashion.

The tax issue is not easy to address. It could well be argued that growing levels of wealth and capital concentration are such a severe risk that state coercion in the form of tax is justified for the purpose of the creation of a community fund. However, Meade's notion that such a fund should be a fundamental redistributive measure owning half of a nation's economic assets would give this particular state agency far too much power and require far too much tax revenue. Given that the UK state, for example, currently owns only around 20% of the nation's economic assets, Meade is at severe risk of drifting back to the very state socialism he hopes to avoid.

It is more in the spirit of a small, distributed economy to see the community fund as maybe one relatively modest measure among a number of others which aim to spread the ownership of capital more widely.

DEMOCRACY UNCORRUPTED

The great fear of the American revolutionaries was that the republican state they had established would become corrupted by the very wealthy. They were all too aware, of course, how generation upon generation of European monarchs had maintained their power only by looking after the economic interests of the land-owning classes. For that reason, maybe more than any other, they were deeply concerned by the rise of a super-rich class that would bend the state to their own interests leaving the less well-off disenfranchised and disengaged at best, or openly hostile to the republic at worst. Because of this, many who came after the revolutionaries also opposed the creation of commercial corporations with special legal privileges, fearing this would create the very class of super-rich organisations and individuals whom leaders like Madison and Jefferson had feared.

Surveying the role that money plays in American politics today, it is impossible to doubt the founding fathers' prescience. More than any other democratic state in an advanced economy, US politics has become a commercial industry awash with billions of corporate dollars, seeking to buy influence through lobbying, party donations, candidate support and public campaigning.

The amount spent on US politics is dizzying. Corporations and other organisations looking to influence Washington dispense around $3.5 billion each year. According to the Center for Responsive Politics[44], the US Chamber of Commerce is by far the biggest spender, shelling out $124 million in 2014 to ensure its members' interests were looked after.

However, individual corporations also splash a great deal of money to get their way. The five biggest corporate spenders paid no less than £823 million between 2009 and 2014 to influence lawmakers in Washington. More cash was involved in the 2012 congressional elections than any previous. Candidates raised $724 billion between them, of which over half came from wealthy individual donors. In the 2012 presidential election campaign Mitt Romney and Barack Obama spent $2.3 billion between them.

The outcome of this system awash with money is predictable. Professors Martin Gilens and Benjamin Page carried out a statistical analysis of 1,779 policy issues dealt with by Washington between 1982 and 2002 to estimate the extent to which the views of the 10% wealthiest Americans and organised lobbying groups fared against the views of middle-income citizens. What they discovered was that money certainly can't get you everything you want in Washington but it definitely helps.

The best way to get a policy or law adopted is undoubtedly for it to have the backing of both the wealthiest and middle earners. But when these groups disagree on a particular policy then the wealthy are much more likely to be victorious. This is particularly the case when the wealthy oppose a particular

---

44   All data can be found on the Center's website: https://www.opensecrets.org/

change. Gilens and Page found that if the richest support a policy or law then its chances of being adopted are about one in two, but if they oppose a change then the likelihood of that change happening falls to about one in five.

In effect, the authors conclude that the wealthiest have a near veto over what gets done in Washington – a recent example being changes to tax on interest payments to hedge fund and private equity bosses. Despite the widespread opposition to arrangements that allowed these very wealthy individuals to pay only 15% tax on their income, efforts in 2012 to close this tax loophole came to nothing.

The sums involved in politics in other advanced economies are tiny by comparison but that does not mean the wealthy have less influence. Parties and candidates need funds and those funds tend to come from the richest individuals and organisations.

Clearly, with such a grip on politics creating a small, distributed economy is no easy task. The ideas proposed in this chapter would seriously damage the interests of very well-off organisations and individuals by reducing their control over corporations, taxing their wealth more heavily and sharing out the capital that is the source of their riches and power far more widely. The extraordinary opposition that emerges when relatively minor changes are suggested to taxing the well-off – such as property taxes in the UK or inheritance taxes in the US – gives only an inkling of the opposition that would emerge to a programme as thoroughgoing as that suggested here.

Of course tighter controls or bans on lobbying and stricter limits on political donations could make a significant difference to the undue influence the well-off have over government. Such moves, however, fail to deal with the fact that the skewed nature of modern politics arises not solely from money but from the way policy and law is set by a group of tightly-knit and overlapping elites operating with great concentrations of political, economic and cultural power. So changing the economy also requires the type of change to the way we do politics, as outlined in previous chapters. We need a shift to a system that gives ordinary people a real say over political decisions at the expense of the undue influence wielded by wealthy individuals and organisations.

The core of the small power vision of the economy is to understand that inequality is not primarily about differences in living standards or life chances, important as these might be. What makes inequality so damaging is that it is an undue concentration of power in the hands of a largely static elite. It limits the enterprise, creativity and freedom of millions by denying them the power and resources to turn their ideas into reality and live as independent, self-determined individuals. It is a particular affront in the 21st century because the tools and the desire for enterprise and self-determination are more widespread than ever before. We now have the chance to accelerate and expand the great strides forward of the last 250 years by rewarding everyone, rather than just a technical or business elite for entrepreneurial, creative behaviour. But we can only do this if wealth is a reward for enterprise rather than for position or birth.

Section IV

SMALL CULTURE:

DEFENDING DIVERSITY

15

Rebellion Against Conformity

THE NUCLEAR FAMILY

By the middle decades of the 20th century, the big power ethos was influencing not just business and government but also culture – the value and behaviours people exhibited in their everyday lives. Just as the totalitarian regimes of Nazi Germany and communist Russia took the big power approach to the economy and the state to its most extreme lengths, so they also made enormous efforts to prescribe how their subjects were to behave in the home, during their leisure time and, most importantly, how they were to think about everything from art to foreign affairs. These aggressive attempts to impose a centrally determined conformity was fictionalised in powerful form in George Orwell's chilling novel 1984, published just four years after the end of the Second World War.

But while the abysmal Soviet regime was Orwell's target, it was no mistake that he set his book in a future England. The dreariness that emerged after the war was largely the result of rationing, which was to continue into the early 1950s, but it also owed something to a new moralism that determined what people should and should not do in their supposedly private lives. Even in America, where economic confidence and living standards bounced back much more rapidly, the same conformist consensus seemed to grip the popular imagination.

That consensus focused on the central importance to society and to the well-being of its citizens of a particular type of family. This was the so-called "nuclear family" – a term that gained popularity in the 1940s not least because of the increasing role that nuclear weapons were playing in international relations. At the heart of the nuclear family was a happy, married heterosexual couple with a well-adjusted brood of children. Gender roles were clearly demarcated with the husband as the head of the household and breadwinner and the wife as carer for the children and guardian of the home. Male children were expected to aspire to a career, girls to get married young and have their own kids.

Homosexuality was particularly derided in a climate that placed such a strong emphasis on a very heterosexual ideal of family life and childrearing. While sex between men had been illegal for decades, the 1940s and 1950s was a particularly difficult time for gay people. As relations between the West and the Soviet Union deteriorated into the Cold War, homosexuality became closely associated in the public mind with communism. Gay men working in government were seen as prone to blackmail by the Soviet secret services, but there was also something about the transgressive nature of gay sex and culture that seemed all part of a dangerous, alien threat to the Western way of life.

It was a perspective that was reinforced when two of the most notorious British Soviet spies of the period, Guy Burgess and John Vassal, were revealed to be gay. Even in the notorious case of the heterosexual couple executed in America for spying, Julius and Ethel Rosenberg, there was the common suggestion in media coverage of the scandal that Julius was unmasculine and dominated by his wife.

This inevitably had an impact on the decisions of those in

authority. In the UK, the Conservative Home Secretary, David Maxwell-Fyfe, urged police and courts to take a tough line on gay sex. The result was that while prosecutions numbered only 299 between 1935 and 1939, the figure rose to 800 for the single year of 1945 and no less than 2,500 in 1955. The climate was so hostile that even the Homosexual Law Reform Society had a policy of only communicating its views via heterosexual spokespeople given the low esteem in which gay people were held.

Ruining the lives of gay men was one thing but interfering in the sexual activity of heterosexuals was a step too far for the democratic governments of the West. This did not prevent, however, cultural norms reinforcing the notion that sex was reserved for the happy couple at the heart of the nuclear family. As such, the hostility towards premarital sex and promiscuity intensified at this time.

The enormously popular novel, *Marjorie Morningstar* written by the American author Herman Wouk, spent 750 pages detailing a young woman's ultimately failed efforts to protect her virginity before marriage. A guide for newly married couples published in 1959 by the British Medical Association was withdrawn after it included a mild suggestion that premarital sex might not be the evil it was made out to be.

Even within marriage there was a vigorous debate about how to ensure the appropriate use of birth control techniques. The National Marriage Guidance Council included in its General Principles, the stern warning that:

> . . . scientific contraception, while serving a purpose in assisting married couples to regulate the spacing of their children, becomes a danger when misused to enable selfish and irresponsible people to escape the duties and disciplines of marriage and parenthood.[45]

---

45 Elizabeth Wilson, *Only Halfway to Paradise*

Benita Eisler, who undertook a study of young adults in the postwar era took a stark perspective: "Of all the secrets of coming of age in the fifties, sex was the darkest and the dirtiest. As sexual beings, people became underground men and women".

Of course, the sanction against premarital sex was applied far more rigorously to young females than it was to young males. This was all a part of a culture of conformity that particularly constrained the role of women to that of housewife and mother – a culture reinforced by the growing corporations.

As the postwar economic boom took off and wages rose rapidly, corporations stepped up their output of mass produced goods and began to invest ever larger amounts into advertising campaigns. This was far more sophisticated marketing than that which existed before the war. Companies realised they were not just selling useful products but aspiration. Owning a car, taking a holiday, filling your new suburban house with "mod cons" were things to which every nuclear family should aspire. Images and text abounded that reinforced the idea that the working man would want to purchase these products to make his wife's daily work easier or to provide a treat for the "little woman" back home. Advertising aimed at women, on the other hand, consistently sought to reassure them that by buying a particular product they could be a more dutiful wife to their husband. The big television networks reinforced the message, churning out dramas and particularly sitcoms that centred on the life of the nuclear family, consistently focused on a working husband and stay-at-home wife.

This constant cultural drumbeat had its effect or, at least, reinforced the conformist sensibilities of the time. Americans began getting married earlier and having children younger. By the end of the 1950s, 70% of all American women were married by the time they were 24 with almost half getting hitched in their teens. The birth rate, which had been declining for a century and half, went into reverse with the number of children being born to the average family rising by 50%. Two-thirds of white women dropped out of college before graduating and the number of women pursuing professional degrees began to decline.[46]

As Wini Breines, the sociologist and 1950s teenager herself, noted, the fear of ending up unmarried and childless was prevalent. A 1955 research study of women's attitudes, for example, found that the phrase "old maid" was extremely commonplace. It explained:

An old maid was a person who had failed so seriously in her understanding or execution of a woman's role that she hadn't even established the marriage prerequisite to having a home. Old maids were not figures of horror so much, or of abhorrence, as they were objects of condescending pity.

Of all the elements of the Big Power Consensus of the 20th century, however, it was the enforcement of cultural conformity that proved the most fragile. The laws and social norms that enforced the consensus were to be severely challenged during the 1960s and 1970s in a far more radical and effective way than the big economic and political consensus. Maybe this should not be a surprise. It is difficult but, nevertheless, far easier to simply refuse to conform to others' expectations than it is to dismantle corporate or governmental structures. But, in truth, the tensions within the big cultural consensus were always powerful.

Despite the stereotyping of the woman as housewife and

---

46 Wini Breines, *Young, White and Miserable*

mother, more women were actually going out to work than ever before in the 1940s and 1950s. In fact, the UK government had encouraged this, to address severe labour shortages. Surveys of family life in the 1950s picked up deep dissatisfaction among women about their restricted roles, their relationships with their husbands and the fact that only junior jobs were available to them. Marriage may have reached a new high but so did divorce. And the comfortable whiteness of the nuclear family was being disturbed by the sight of civil rights campaigners demanding equality while facing brutality from the supposed upstanding, decent men of this new America.

As Wini Breines says: ". . . the young, white, middle-class women who grew up in the midst of these contradictions were dry tinder for the spark of revolt".

OUT AND PROUD

By the 1960s a new generation was rejecting the sexual constraints of the nuclear family. Film, theatre and television became more daring and challenging of accepted values. Pop music became a focus for youthful rebellion against the suburban conformist values of the postwar era. At the same time, the civil rights movement led by Martin Luther King was reaching the height of its influence, shaking the complacent racism of the period.

The violence directed against civil rights campaigners and the shocking images from the Vietnam War appearing daily on television news broadcasts helped turn this cultural rebellion into something far more political by the later years of the decade. Students in rapidly expanding universities across Europe and America embraced the revolutionary ideals of Karl Marx and others. Their rebellions against old-fashioned university authorities soon turned into wider rebellions against capitalism and war. Demonstrations, sometimes violent, became increasingly regular occurrences, ultimately resulting in the May events of 1968 when universities across Europe were occupied by students, and part of Paris fell briefly out of the control of the police as students rioted and erected barricades.

A large number of young women were enthusiastic participants in this radical upsurge, but many of them discovered that their own demands to be treated as equals within these movements were barely given a second thought by the confident young men leading the campaigns. As one activist put it, women were at best seen as "worker ant type people" there to paint the banners, make the coffee and soothe the egos of their brave street-fighting men. At worst, they were ridiculed and abused when they tried to challenge such attitudes.

The emerging leader of a new generation of civil rights campaigners, Stokeley Carmichael, summed up the attitude of many radical young men when he was asked what the position of women should be in the movement: "Prone," he replied.

Supposed hotbeds of alternative thought and action such as the Students for a Democratic Society group showed the limits of their radicalism when women calling for a focus on their rights and concerns at a conference were pelted with food and driven from the stage. Similar attempts to block discussion or progress on women's rights were repeated in organisations across the world wherever the student radical movement had taken hold.

For gay men involved in the politics of the 1960s, the challenge was more subtle but no less problematic. While women fighting for rights and recognition faced hostility and ridicule, gay men faced a wall of indifference. Gay rights were simply not seen as a significant issue. These movements were fighting for "important" things like an end to imperial aggression or working class revolution, not the right to express yourself sexually. (Unless you were a heterosexual man, of course, in which case free love was a deeply revolutionary act.)

Part of the reason for the indifference was that gay men themselves largely accepted this point of view. Until the early 1970s gay sexuality was simply not seen as a political issue. It was something to be kept private. But that didn't stop a growing sense that something was wrong here. As one British activist put it, there was a strengthening feeling that gay men were being left out of all the "love-in-the-mud" fun. Despite their commitment to the campaigns of the 1960s, there was a part of the gay activist that had to remain hidden if they were to maintain the respect of their comrades and friends.

Maybe if gay men had been as vocal as women about their demands they may have faced the same opposition. That was certainly the experience of gay women. When a group of lesbians demanded that the campaign group, the National Organisation of Women, take up their concerns, they met a very frosty response. Betty Friedan, the formidable President of NOW, rejected lesbianism as a "lavender menace" that would destroy the credibility of the women's movement, and she made it her goal to expel lesbian activists from the organisation.

What women, gay men and lesbians were discovering was that the big culture emphasis on conventional "family" values was not just an invention of the 1940s and 1950s. The message may have intensified in those decades, but it was built on prejudices and taboos stretching back millennia. It would require far more challenging and bolder movements to break that big culture and allow diversity and personal choice to flourish than could be provided by the 1960s radicals. It was this insight that made the 12 months of 1970 the beginning of the end for the era of big culture. In that year, radical movements for women's and gay people's freedom burst into action and public prominence.

On 26th August, the 50th anniversary of the women's suffrage amendment, a Women's Strike for Equality Day was held, with marches across the US. For many Americans it was their first exposure to a new, forthright movement called "feminism". It kick-started a sudden explosion of interest in, and support for, women's rights and freedoms. The National Organisation of Women saw their membership grow from 4,000 in 1970 to 20,000 in 1973, and then 125,000 by the end of the decade. The Women's Equity Action League, which had split from the National Organisation of Women to represent women in the professions, expanded rapidly to 40 state chapters.[47]

In the UK, women campaigners decided to do something somewhat more eye-catching. In November, the annual Miss World beauty contest was being held in London. Established in 1951 when the nuclear family conformity was at its height, Miss World was televised live across the globe on major television networks securing audiences in the hundreds of millions. What the organisers did not know was that a group of campaigners had bought tickets for the show. When the compere, the well-known American comic Bob Hope, began his opening monologue, the women began blowing whistles, running down the aisles and onto the stage shouting, "We're not beautiful, we're not ugly, we're angry". The protestors explained afterwards that they simply wanted the freedom to develop their own identity without being judged, literally in the case of Miss World, by men. The publicity around the stunt, the trial of five of the protestors and a large follow-up demonstration grabbed the attention of thousands of women who set up at least 80 local women's groups across the UK by the end of 1971.

This campaigning activity was accompanied by an explosion

---

47   Kathleen Berkeley, *The Women's Liberation Movement in America*

of publishing, with new magazines, newspapers and books aimed directly at the women's movement, suddenly appearing. In 1970 alone, three classic feminist texts were published and devoured enthusiastically by women joining this new movement: *Sisterhood is Powerful* edited by Robin Morgan, *The Dialectic of Sex: The Case for a Feminist Revolution* by Shulamith Firestone and *Sexual Politics* by Kate Millett.

A similar explosion of activity seized gay campaigners as well. On 28th June 1970, gay men and women congregated to hold a rally in New York, demanding their rights and freedom. Other demonstrations had been held before but this was different. Thousands rather than dozens attended and this time it was angry. The reason was simple – the rally took place on the street where the year prior hundreds of gay people had rioted after their patience had finally snapped following yet another police raid on the Stonewall bar – a popular meeting place for gay men.

The riot had tripped something in the minds of thousands of young gay men and women across America who felt alienated not just by the attitude of mainstream society but also the radical political movements in which many had been involved. Two new organisations sprang up in the weeks immediately after the riot – the Gay Liberation Front and the Gay Activists' Alliance – and rapidly attracted supporters across the country. The 1970 demonstration drew the attention of the world to this new movement and the world reacted. In the UK, two students at the London School of Economics – which had been at the epicentre of 1960s student rebellion in the UK – decided to set up their own Gay Liberation Front in October. The first meeting attracted 20 people. Within weeks, hundreds were attending.

This explosion of radicalism in 1970 was not the first time campaigns had been launched for women's and gay rights. In fact, many brave people had been striving since the mid-1950s to challenge the ingrained prejudice that restricted the freedom of choice of women and gay people. But these campaigns were conducted in very polite terms as though the campaigners feared annoying those they were trying to influence.

But after a decade of social and political rebellion, women and gay people no longer felt the need to secure the respect of those who enforced the big cultural values of the postwar period. A deliberate decision was taken by this new generation of activists to simply behave as they wanted.

So the most liberating feature of this period was not campaigns for complex legal changes but the sudden freedom to be who you wanted to be alongside others who felt the same. For many young gay men and women, the most revolutionary aspect of the new movement was not the demonstrations and leafletting but the organisation of discos where gay people could gather together openly and proudly. No more furtive, dingy bars or, worse, lives lived out in denial of one's own real sexuality. This is why "coming out" rapidly became such an important part of the movement and has been central to gay people's lives ever since.

For women, the attendance at women's groups was also a liberation in itself. For the first time many discovered that the frustration and anger they felt at being trapped in their pre-ordained nuclear family role was not something peculiar to them. Other women, and many of them, felt exactly the same way. The slogan "the personal is political" caught on in the women's movement because so many women were discovering that their frustration was not the result of personal failings on their part, as the big postwar culture had implied, but because a certain set of social and political values had forced them into roles they found frustrating and demeaning.

This was a very practical and immediate way of dismantling the postwar culture and encouraging, in its place, a world where individuals were free to make decisions about their lives for themselves. And the impact spread rapidly beyond the realms of politically motivated campaigners. A survey of American female college students in 1971 found that only 23% saw the main purpose of their college course as career development. No less than 18% believed that college was primarily about getting ready for marriage and family life. Only nine years later, 40% were at college to prepare for careers while just 1% saw it as preparation for marriage.[48]

A big conformist vision where everyone lived similar lives bounded by a narrow set of accepted behaviours began to collapse into a world of small culture where people set their own rules and determined their own behaviours without reference to a big controlling body. The rebellion of the 1960s certainly played a role in this, but it was the liberation movements of the 1970s that went to the very heart of that big culture built around the nuclear family and its values, and stopped it dead.

---

48   Kathleen Berkeley, *The Women's Liberation Movement in America*

16

Taking on the Control Freaks

On 22nd May 2015 something truly remarkable happened in the history of the battle between small and big power. On that day Ireland voted to make same sex marriage legal. What was striking, however, about the decision was that it was made not by a parliament or a court as had been the case in all other countries but by a popular vote of the Irish people. And it was no close-run thing – the referendum voted for the change by 62% to 38%.

This was a striking embrace by the whole population of one nation of the principles behind small cultural power: diversity and freedom of choice. And it was all the more striking for happening in Ireland, a country that had for centuries had its morals and its laws deeply shaped by the conformist, big cultural power mindset of the Catholic Church. Indeed, the Church had vigorously opposed the change during the referendum campaign. A very senior Vatican official described the decision of the Irish people as a "defeat for humanity".

Less than 50 years after the first brick was thrown against police outside the Stonewall Bar in New York, numerous countries across the world have moved from punishing gay sex by imprisonment to opening the most sacred social institution of marriage to gay and lesbian couples. As numerous surveys show, this legal shift reflects deep changes in how populations view gay people – from one of deep disapproval or pity to one of acceptance and support in their fight against discrimination.

Nowhere is this clearer than in many areas of popular culture. It is now largely unremarkable for a television series to include one or more gay characters or for pop stars and actors to be completely open about their sexuality. Compare this, for example, with the furore that greeted the inclusion of a gay character in the popular American sitcom Soap in the late 1970s, with religious and right wing groups campaigning for the show to be cancelled, or efforts at the same time by Christian groups in the UK to close down the newspaper *Gay News*. This transformation in the conditions under which gay people live is replicated for other groups.

The sexist model of the nuclear family, which became such a powerful force for cultural and social conformity in the postwar period, has lost its resonance and power. The notion that a woman's place is in the home, providing unquestioning service to her breadwinner husband has been overtaken by the reality of millions of women taking jobs, securing an education and, maybe most importantly, expecting and often fighting for the same freedoms, status and rewards available to men.

The casual racism of the postwar period, which saw black people disenfranchised from political and education systems, marginalised in the economy and national cultures, is now weaker than it ever was. The legal segregation of the southern US states has been dismantled; black celebrities are commonplace and in some cases now the most recognisable and richest people in their industries. Black people now expect and fight for the same rights as white people.

The notion that disabled people should be treated as medical cases requiring "treatment" within large, hierarchical healthcare facilities has been discredited. It is now extremely common for public services and civil society organisations to work with disabled people to enable them to lead independent lives. The growing global popularity of the Paralympics speaks eloquently of a world that has moved from seeing the disabled as objects of pity or embarrassment to one of celebration and adulation.

This is a much "smaller" world than existed even 20 years ago. The big cultural power that insisted on removing choice and dignity from those who were different from the homogenous ideal of the white, heterosexual, able-bodied family man is now incalculably weaker than it was. The result is more diverse societies where cultural power increasingly operates at the level of the individual rather than the big hierarchical organisation.

It shows what can be achieved in the space of one generation when determined people with a small power vision campaign ceaselessly and fearlessly for a different world. It reveals what could be won if the same determination was applied to the worlds of the economy and politics where big power institutions still dominate.

BIG CULTURAL POWER FIGHTS BACK

But if the history teaches us anything, it is that progress towards small power can always be reversed. Those who benefit from and believe in big power rarely miss an opportunity to reduce the free choice of their fellow humans. Even though the battles for diversity and freedom are far from over in the advanced economies – and have barely begun in some other parts of the world – those who wish to impose conformity through hierarchical control are already pushing back.

The biggest threat to the cultural small power gains of the last 40 years now originates with the rise of populist politics across Europe and the US. These parties and organisations, which had been gradually building support for a number of years, received a significant boost following the 2008 crash, the long recession and, in Europe, the Eurozone crisis.

Jobbik is now the third largest party in the Hungarian parliament and secured over 20% of the vote in the 2014 parliamentary election. The Leader of the Front National in France, Marine Le Pen, came third in the country's 2012 presidential election. In the French local elections in March 2015, the FN got more first preference votes than any other party with a quarter of the total vote. Sweden Democrats has doubled its vote at every parliamentary election since 1998 and, at the time of writing, polls suggest it now has more support than any other party. The *Economist* magazine recently noted 22 European countries where similar populist parties were growing in support and influence.[49]

In America, this strand has taken the form of the Tea Party, which has exerted a powerful influence over the Republican Party for a number of years and spread its message through well-known radio and TV personalities. Most recently, this populist perspective found its expression through the high profile presidential bid of Donald Trump.

These populist parties are not homogenous. Some antiestablishment populist messages can even seem aligned with small power. Elements in The Tea Party, for example, are hostile to big business and cronyism in government and claim to speak up on behalf of small-scale entrepreneurs. The UK Independence Party, like a number of other populist parties across Europe, argues for a more direct democracy, which bears some similarities to the political ideas outlined in this book. Then there are parties like Golden Dawn in Greece, which are fascistic, or Front National in France, which are political authoritarians.

---

49   *Europe's Populist Insurgents – Turning Right:* http://econ.st/1bLxyo6

But as Matthew Goodwin, an academic expert on populism, points out, they all share a "core characteristic . . . they
fiercely oppose . . . rising ethnic and cultural diversity".

This is the threat they pose to the small cultural power
advances of the last few decades. While many of these parties
may offer a façade of respectability and modernity, the deep
hostility to people who differ from their perception of what is
normal is never far from the surface. The UK Independence
Party, for example, has been plagued by a long series of
unguarded racist, homophobic and sexist comments by senior
party figures and activists. The party also made its opposition
to gay marriage a key feature of its election campaign in 2015.
The Jobbik Party in Hungary regularly has to counter clear
examples of its own antisemitism and has made hostility to the
country's Roma community a major element in its electoral
campaigns. Golden Dawn barely makes an effort to hide its
admiration for the genocidal Third Reich and even regularly
sings the German Nazi Party anthem at its rallies.

It is also telling that the Tea Party, for all their complex and
conflicting strands and views, had by 2015 boiled their message down to one of intemperate hostility to Latino and
Muslim immigration represented by Donald Trump. Maybe
this should not be surprising. Alan Abramowitz, an academic
who has studied the Tea Party, found that many of its supporters were characterised both by an intense conservatism and
racial hostility.

Whether these parties secure positions of significant political power is up for debate. They generally thrive on simply
being the focus for visceral protest against mainstream politics.
Taking on positions of power with all the compromises and
complexities that entails would likely damage that important
element of their appeal to supporters. Indeed, the Austrian
Freedom Party – an early example of this version of populism
– went into a coalition government in 2000 only to experience

serious internal divisions and a loss of over half of its votes by the next election.

Nevertheless, what this upsurge of support for populism can do is shift public opinion and the centre ground of political debate towards a less tolerant big cultural power perspective. France, for example, has seen governments harden their position on Muslim cultural practices, under pressure from the rise of the Front National. In 2011, a law was passed making it illegal to wear full face coverings in public places. Although in theory, this was deemed a security measure to allow identification by police and other authorities, it was clear from the nature of the debate that preceded the measure, that it was aimed primarily at the very small minority of Muslim women who wear the burka or full niqab.

One can see a similar process in the US where the huge attention given to Donald Trump and his strong support among the party's grassroots has forced other Republican contenders for the presidential nomination to shift their position towards Trump's big cultural power agenda, particularly on the immigration issue and attitudes towards Latinos and Muslims.

The risk must be that the longer these political forces secure significant support within Europe and the US, the more likely it is that they will ultimately succeed in imposing their agenda on mainstream parties and governments. They will also risk becoming more ambitious, launching campaigns to drive back gains or prevent further advances for women, gay people and black people. As we know from history, such reverses are far from uncommon even if they seem unlikely at a time when a small power mindset prevails.

The solution has two parts. The first is to keep on campaigning and fighting proudly to protect the changes of the last four decades and to advance them further. The history in this book shows conclusively that only such bold and forceful action ultimately secures the necessary defeat of those in thrall to big power cultural values who see only one valid way of living life. Ignoring the rise of big power forces, however marginal they may seem, is never a solution.

The second is to recognise that much of the attraction of populism lies in the intense alienation from representative democratic systems that has swept across Europe and the US. Research studying voters who back populist parties finds that while it may not be the sole factor in their support, it is certainly a highly significant or the most significant factor. Forty-eight per cent of the general public in the UK may think politicians are "out merely for themselves" rather than doing what's best for the country but this rises to a striking 74% among those who vote for the UK Independence Party. Major surveys show similar levels of disaffection with established political institutions among supporters of populist parties in other European countries.

The more that mainstream parties ape the new extremists the higher the likelihood that the small culture advances of the last four decades will be reversed or, at the very best, will come to a halt. Those parties must recognise that the way to address this alienation is to move towards the more direct, deliberative system of democratic government discussed earlier. This is what those who are alienated with the current state of politics repeatedly tell researchers they want to see. This will not necessarily reduce the deep desire some always seem to have to marginalise and control those who are different but it would deny these parties of one of their most important ways to recruit support.

Changes in law and political culture are required so that elected representatives have no choice but to put the views of the people who elect them first. It should become the norm that on all of the big issues of the day, members of parliaments have well-established, well-resourced and rigorous processes for engaging their constituents in detailed online and offline deliberation and decision-making. And whatever consensus emerges should constitute the view promoted by that representative in their parliamentary chamber within the context of the attempt to build a wider national consensus.

Only such a transformation will engage the millions who feel cut out of their nation's decision-making by big, concentrated power. Only such a transformation will stop the populists who cynically exploit profound political frustration dead in their tracks.

Conclusion – small power: out and proud

A WORLD OF CONFUSION

Our world is going through an intense period of transition. Populations across the world increasingly value the small power ideals of self-expression, free choice and diversity, and yet the big power institutions created in the last century cling on.

As this book has explained, there are many troubling outcomes from this tension. But one effect is confusion. This is particularly important when considering the prospects for the creation of a small power world. The ideologies that shape our public debates and the way politicians speak have become extremely muddled.

On the one hand, there are left-leaning parties and organisations, which fervently favour the small power revolution that has occurred in the cultural sphere, actively supporting gay rights, antiracism and feminism. Indeed, many on the left proudly see themselves as part of a long history of antiestablishment battles, which have pitted "ordinary" people of limited power against an establishment of big corporate and governmental forces.

And yet this is the same left that almost uniformly rushes to the defence of big state structures in the form of top-down welfare and public services. It rejects, or is at least very suspicious of, any attempt to cut government spending. It increasingly displays nostalgia for the big state established in the 20th century with vigorous attempts since the 2008 crash to revive Keynesian models, tougher regulation of business practices and economic planning.

Most confusingly, this is a political strand which regularly sets its face against the abuses committed by oligopolistic corporations and yet is increasingly enamoured by the creation of even bigger, monopolistic corporations in the form of state-owned enterprises.

However, the right of the political spectrum is no less confused. Since the 1980s and the ideological revolution led by Ronald Reagan and Margaret Thatcher, the right claims to be the political wing that most values the small power ideals of individual free choice and enterprise. As a result, their focus has been on reducing the size and power of the state to free people and businesses from regulation and political control. And yet, when it comes to individual free choice in cultural and social matters, there is more virulent opposition on the right than anywhere else. The Republican Party in the US seems to be defined as much by its hostility to antiracism, gay rights and feminism as by its opposition to the big state. Right wing populists across Europe offer a mix of antistate, free market principles combined with demands for the state to exercise its power to control the cultural and religious practices of minority groups, as well as the free choice of gay people and women.

And while the right opposes the undue domination of governments over individual citizens, they seem far less willing to condemn the dominance that big business exerts over the economy. Nor do they question the way increasing inequality gives an ever smaller group enormous political, economic and cultural power that ultimately undermines the goal of rewarding individual enterprise.

This book has argued that there has never been a better time to promote small power values. People are more entrepreneurial, better educated and more creative than they have ever been. Giving people the freedom to make their own creative choices, while rewarding them with esteem and money for the actions that lead to a better, more fulfilling world, could underpin a new unmatched era of human progress.

On the other hand, a failure to embrace small power by maintaining the death grip exerted by the big power institutions of the last century will only create greater tension and conflict of the sort already emerging in the form of populist politics. However, this small power revolution will not happen by accident. The ideological confusion that grips our political classes and reinforces big power while proclaiming itself for small power, needs to be challenged.

A MOMENT OF HISTORIC CLARITY

What is required is an out and proud movement led by small power values which unashamedly demands self-determination and self-expression for all of us in every aspect of our lives. The pick and mix approach to big and small power that currently infects our political spectrum stands in the way of such a thoroughgoing vision. Small power must run through every area in the forms of the three Ds: direct, distributed, diverse.

First, we need to dismantle the elite, hierarchical power that politicians and public officials have come to exert over our lives. That means a radical shift towards systems that give us a more *direct* say over our governments and the services they provide. Our representatives should be required to listen to the views of their electors and put them before those of party leaders, wealthy donors and lobbyists or the media when deciding on major issues. We also need to move as much as possible to a system where tax funds are taken out of the hands of public officials and are instead given directly to the service users to spend as they see fit in line with their own personal needs.

Second, a small power vision must include a fairer *distribution* of economic reward and resources in our economy. Although the 20th century mechanisms of tax and spend have a role to play in this, they have now reached a stage where their growth imperils the health of economies and where they are generating diminishing social returns. Instead, the rules and norms that govern our economy must be shifted so that financial rewards genuinely flow to the millions of workers and consumers who contribute to innovation and growth in an era where entrepreneurial and creative behaviours are much more widespread.

That means that the established structure of a corporation, that sees most of a firm's wealth returned to big investors, needs to be rethought so employees and customers can also be fully rewarded. Home ownership must become an affordable aspiration again, not through grandiose plans of government led building schemes but simply by dismantling the planning and zoning restrictions, which helps the rich get richer and stops the market doing its job. The oligopolies that dominate the global economy need to be broken up to allow small business and a wider distribution of wealth to flourish. And the burden of tax must shrink but also shift from trade and employment and towards those big concentrations of wealth held by families and organisations.

Finally, we need a forceful defence and extension of free choice and *diversity* in our cultural and social lives. The changes in law and in public attitudes of the last 40 years that have dismantled the big cultural consensus of the 20th century must be noisily defended against the new control freaks building political support across Europe and the US. In fact, despite the nonsense spoken by those new political forces, there is still a great deal of work that must be done to ensure that the power to exercise free choice over your own life is as profound and irreversible as it can be for women, black people, gay people, the disabled and a wide range of other groups.

The greatest moment in the past when small power became self-conscious and turned decades of tension between an emerging new world and a crumbling old world into a movement for transformation was the rise of Radicalism in the second half of the 18th century. This was a force for self-determination and self-expression that challenged elites and hierarchy long before big power re-emerged in the late 19th century.

As a result, the Radicals knew instinctively and without confusion that human freedom was indivisible. They made no artificial, academic separation between the political, the economic and the cultural – they opposed monarchs, land-owning aristocrats and priests in equal measure. They saw that free choice had to operate in all spheres if it was to operate in any one.

We desperately need a similar moment of clarity now.

Further Reading

Below are books, papers and articles that have been used as sources throughout *Small is Powerful* and which the readers may find useful should they wish to explore some of the themes and thinkers in the book in more depth.

CHAPTER 2: A GREAT FACT

Eric Beinhocker, *The Origin of Wealth: Evolution, Complexity and the Radical Remaking of Economics*

Adam Lent, *Generation Enterprise: The Hope for a Brighter Economic Future* (The Royal Society of the Arts paper)

Angus Maddison, *The World Economy: Historical Statistics*

Deirdre McCloskey, *Bourgeois Dignity: Why Economics Can't Explain the Modern World*

William Nordhaus, *Do Real-Output and Real-Wage Measures Capture Reality?* in Timothy Bresnahan and Robert Gordon, *The Economics of New Goods*

Roy Porter, *English Society in the Eighteenth Century*

CHAPTER 3: BIG GOVERNMENT BEGINS

Perry Anderson, *Lineages of the Absolutist State*

Martin van Creveld, *The Rise and Decline of the State*

Diarmaid MacCulloch, *Reformation: Europe's House Divided*
Quentin Skinner, *Hobbes and Republican Liberty*
Richard Tuck, *Hobbes: A Very Short Introduction*

CHAPTER 4: RADICAL AMERICA

Joseph Blasi, Richard Freeman and Douglas Kruse, *The Citizen's Share: Putting Ownership Back into Democracy*
Drew McCoy, *The Elusive Republic: Political Economy in Jeffersonian America*
Gottlieb Mittelberger, *Journey to Pennsylvania in the Year 1750, and Return to Germany in the Year 1754*
Sheila Simon, *Odd Couple of the Constitution: James Madison and Alexander Hamilton*
H. Russell Smith, *Harrington and his Oceana*
Gordon Wood, *The Radicalism of the American Revolution*

CHAPTER 5: EUROPE ABLAZE

Edmund Fawcett, *Liberalism: The Life of an Idea*
Robert Gildea, *Barricades and Borders: Europe 1800–1914*
Paul Hirst, *Associative Democracy: New Forms of Economic and Social Governance*
George Lichtheim, *A Short History of Socialism*
Peter Marshall, *Demanding the Impossible: A History of Anarchism*
Clare Tomalin, *The Life and Death of Mary Wollstonecraft*

CHAPTER 6: GOVERNMENT GETS VERY BIG

Alec Cairncross, *The British Economy Since 1945*
Martin van Creveld, *The Rise and Decline of the State*
Robert Skidelsky, *John Maynard Keynes: Economist, Philosopher, Statesman*

Michael Stewart, *Keynes and After*
Vito Tanzi, *Government Versus Markets: The Changing Economic Role of the State*
Jim Tomlinson, *Public Policy and the Economy since 1900*

CHAPTER 7: ZOMBIE POLITICS

Martin van Creveld, *The Rise and Decline of the State*
Moisés Naím, *The End of Power*
The Power Inquiry, *Power to the People: An Independent Inquiry into Britain's Democracy*
Robert Self, *The Evolution of the British Party System 1885–1940*
Paul Whiteley, *Political Participation in Britain: The Decline and Revival of Civic Culture*

CHAPTER 8: LET US HAVE OUR SAY!

Douglas Carswell, *The End of Politics and the Birth of iDemocracy*
The Power Inquiry, *Power to the People: An Independent Inquiry into Britain's Democracy*
Amy Gutmann and Dennis Thompson, *Why Deliberative Democracy?*
Graham Smith, *Democratic Innovations: Designing Institutions for Citizen Participation*

CHAPTER 9: LET US CHOOSE!

Seán Boyle, *Health Systems in Transition (UK)*, European Observatory on Health Systems and Policies
Alex Fox, *Personalisation: Lessons from Social Care* (a RSA paper)

Alex Fox, *People Powered NHS* (a RSA paper)

Julian Le Grand, *The Other Invisible Hand: Delivering Public Services Through Choice and Competition*

Adam Lent, *British Social Movements Since 1945: Sex, Colour, Peace and Power*

Adam Lent, *Making Choices: How Can Choice Improve Local Public Services* (a New Local Government Network paper)

Mike Oliver and Jane Campbell, *Disability Politics: Understanding Our Past, Changing Our Future*

CHAPTER 10: THE RISE OF BIG BUSINESS

John Benson, *The Rise of the Consumer Society in Britain 1880–1980*

Joseph Blasi, Richard Freeman and Douglas Kruse, *The Citizen's Share: Putting Ownership Back into Democracy*

Alec Cairncross, *The British Economy Since 1945*

Alfred Chandler, *The Visible Hand: The Managerial Revolution in American Business*

Patrick Gaughan, *Mergers, Acquisitions and Corporate Restructurings*

Naomi Lamoreaux, *The Great Merger Movement in American Business*

Geoffrey Owen, *From Empire to Europe: The Decline and Revival of British Industry Since the Second World War*

Charles Perrow, *Organizing America: Wealth, Power and the Origins of Corporate Capitalism*

CHAPTER 11: BIG ECONOMIC POWER CHALLENGED

Anthony Atkinson, *Inequality: What Can Be Done?*

Alan Ebenstein, *Friedrich Hayek: A Biography*

Paul Freiberger and Michael Swaine, *Fire in the Valley: The Making of the Personal Computer*

Steven Levy, *Hackers: Heroes of the Computer Revolution*

Thomas Piketty, *Capital in the Twenty-First Century*

E.F. Schumacher, *Small is Beautiful: Economics as if People Mattered*

Barbara Wood, *E.F. Schumacher: His Life and Thought*

CHAPTER 12: EVERYONE AN ENTREPRENEUR

Henry Chesborough, *Open Innovation: The New Imperative for Creating and Profiting from Technology*

Benedict Dellot, *Salvation In a Start-up? The Origins and Nature of the Self-employment Boom* (a RSA paper)

Jesus Huerta de Soto, *The Austrian School: Market Order and Entrepreneurial Creativity*

Frederic Laloux, *Reinventing Organisations: A Guide to Creating Organizations Inspired by the Next Stage of Human Consciousness*

Adam Lent, *Generation Enterprise: The Hope for a Brighter Economic Future* (a RSA paper)

Joseph Pine, *Mass Customisation: The New Frontier in Business Competition*

Doc Searls, *The Intention Economy: When Customers Take Charge*

Christian Welzel, *Freedom Rising: Human Empowerment and the Quest for Emancipaton*

CHAPTER 13: A NOT SO GOLDEN ISLE

Anthony Atkinson, *Inequality: What Can Be Done?*

Miles Corak, *Income Inequality, Equality of Opportunity, and Intergenerational Mobility* (University of Ottawa Discussion Paper)

John Foster, Robert McChesney and R. Jamil Jonna, "Monopoly and Competition in Twenty-First Century Capitalism" in *Monthly Review* April 2011

Barry Lynne, *Cornered: The New Monopoly Capitalism and the Economics of Destruction*

Thomas Piketty, *Capital in the Twenty-First Century*

Maurice Saatchi, *The Road from Serfdom* (a Centre for Policy Studies paper)

CHAPTER 14: UNLEASHING SMALL ECONOMIC POWER

Jonathan Baker and Steven Salop, *Antitrust, Competition Policy, and Inequality* (working paper for American University Washington College of Law)

Angela Cummine, "A Citizen's Income and Wealth Fund for the UK: Lessons from Alaska" in *Juncture* 2015

Liveo Di Matteo, *Measuring Government in the 21st Century: An International Overview of the Size and Efficiency of Public Spending* (a Fraser Institute paper)

Will Davies, *Reinventing the Firm* (a Demos paper)

Richard Florida *et al*, *Creativity and Prosperity: The Global Creativity Index* (a Martin Prosperity Institute paper)

Martin Gilens and Benjamin Page, *Testing Theories of American Politics: Elites, Interest Groups, and Average Citizens* (a Princeton University paper)

Peter Lindert, "Three Centuries of Inequality in Britain and America" in Anthony Atkinson and Francois Bourguignon, *Handbook of Income Distribution*

James Meade, *Agathatopia*

CHAPTER 15: REBELLION AGAINST CONFORMITY

Kathleen C. Berkeley, *The Women's Liberation Movement in America*

Wini Breines, *Young, White and Miserable: Growing Up Female in the Fifties*

Vicki Eaklor, *Queer America: A People's GLBT History of the United States*

Benita Eisler, *Private Lives: Men and Women of the Fifties*

Adam Lent, *British Social Movements Since 1945: Sex, Colour, Peace and Power*

Arthur Marwick, *The Sixties: Cultural Revolution in Britain, France, Italy and the USA*

Arthur Marwick, *British Society Since 1945*

Elizabeth Wilson, *Only Halfway to Paradise: Women in Postwar Britain*

CHAPTER 16: TAKING ON THE CONTROL FREAKS

Alan Abramowitz *Partisan Polarization and the Rise of the Tea Party Movement*

Claudia Chwalisz, *The Populist Signal: Why Politics and Democracy Need to Change* (a Policy Network paper)

Matthew Goodwin, *Right Response: Understanding and Countering Populist Extremism in Europe* (a Chatham House paper)

Anthony Painter, *Democratic Stress, the Populist Signal and Extremist Threat* (a Policy Network paper)

Index

Supporters

Tuna Acar
David Archer
Peter Ashby FRSA
James Aylett
Karen Badenoch
Robin Baker
Nicola Balkind
Arturo Barone
Lily Barton
Matthew Bate
Adam Baylis-West
Dan Bayliss
Andrew Beale
Richard Best
Trevor Best
Dirk Bollen
Bill Bonwitt
Ron Bowd
Claire Bowles
Susannah Bradley
Richard W H Bray
Steve Broome
Malcolm Brown
Matt Brown

Tony Browne
David Bryan
Anthony Bunge
Christopher Burgahn
Dan Burgess
Paul Burgess
Jeremy Burke
Tom Burke
Ed Cadwallader
Matthew Cain
Emily Campbell
Xander Cansell
Tony Cantafio
Kevin Carroll
Mamading Ceesay and
    Sofia Bustamante
Hao Chen
Rathika Chinnadurai
Kelly Clark
David Claydon
Richard Clifford
Dr. Raymond Coffer
Tony Cohen
Steve Coles

Stevyn Colgan
Lee Collins FRSA
Dave Conroy
Alan Constantine
Graeme Cooke
Jamie Cooke
Judit Csapo
Andrew Curry
Robin Curtis
Gerard Darby
Geoffrey Darnton
Sevra Davis
Floyd DCosta
Benedict Dellot
Roanne Dods
Tony Dolphin
Kevin Donnellon
Paul Driver
Tiffany Duggan
Dave Dyke
David Easton
Uche Eke
Zoë Elder
Katy Evans
Julien Fayet
Mark Ferguson
Vicky Ferrier
Kim Fitzpatrick
David Floyd
Simon Gruffydd Foster
Alex Fox
Dan Fox
Laura Fox
Aldo Framingo

Isobel Frankish
Olly Freedman
John Frewin
Dominic Frisby
FrolleinFlow
Hilary Gallo
Mark Gamble
Richard Paul Gamblin
Lisa Gansky
Andy Gardiner
Bill Gibbon
Patrick Gibson
Martin Gilbraith
Richard Given
Maklab Glasgow
Bill & Erika Gloyn
Gerlinde Gniewosz
Mathias Goldmann
Carl Gombrich
Philip Gosling
Ian Greatorex
Alex Griffiths
Neil Grosse
William Hackett-Jones
Iain Hallam
Anders Sahl Hansen
Joy Harris
Barry Harvey
Allan Hayes
Paul Hayes
Chris Haynes
Andrew Hearse
John Herbert
Bonnie Hewson

Robert Hill
Geoffrey Hodgson
Loretta Hoffmann
Valerie Holden
Janice Holve
Todd Hoskins
Catherine Howe
Dan Howe
David Huber
Darren Hughes
Patrick Hughes
David Huntley
Virginia Schumacher
  Isaac
Johari Ismail
Nicolas Janssen
Erin Johnson
Luke Johnson
Aled Jones
Liz Darcy Jones
Jamie Joseph
Keith Kahn-Harris
Gareth Kay
Andrew Kelly
Steve Kelsey
Hilary Kemp
Robert the mason Kemp
Dan Kieran
Shadiya Kingerlee
Philipp Paul Köhler
Satu Korhonen
Kim Korn
Raj Kosaraju
Alex Kovach

Elsie L'Huillier
Tom LaForge
Rob Lamond
Stewart Lansley
Paul Laviers
Patricia Lawlor
Carl Lens
Carol Lent
Matt Lent
Penny Lent
Josef Lentsch
Robert Leonard
Guy Levin
Jari Liitola
Alisa Lindsay
Karen Loasby
Jack Lord
Michael Macdonald
Lucy Macnab
Martin Mahaux
Harinder Mann
Keith Mantell
Alex Marsh
Wendy Martineau
Jeff Masters
Ash Matadeen
Richard Mayston
Colleen McCulloch
Brendan McLoughlin
Alison Bond McNally
Martin McTague
Michael McTernan
William Mehornay
Richard Merrick

Yang Meyer
Emran Mian
Andy Middleton
Peter Milburn
Greg Moffitt
Nicola Morelli
Bronwen Morgan
Simon Morioka
Amanda Muckalt
Rick Muir
Elisabeth Murdoch
Lilly Murmann
Alicia Murray
Ebi Nafis
Araz Najarian
David Narciso
David Nash
Carlo Navato
John Naylor
Mark Newey
John O'Brien
K Eric O'Callaghan
Brendan O'Grady
Edward Kevin O'Hara
Adam Ogilvie
Virpi Oinonen
Gwyn Owen
Anthony Painter
Nick Parker
James Parry
Åsmund Paulsen
Nick Pearce
Carlota Perez
David Perry

Steven Phillips
Sean Pillot de Chenecey
Sacha Platteeuw
Stephen Plumridge
James Plunkett
Justin Pollard
Roman Pope
Jan M Portillo
Wendy Potter
Joe Powell
Tony Curzon Price
Graham Randles
Howard Reed
Oliver Reichardt
Gillian Reynolds
Steve Richards
Paull Robathan
Nan Roberts
Ian Roderick
Gerald Rothman
Elizabeth Rowlands
Chris Ryan
Martin Ryan
Ruth Sack
Christoph Sander
Matthew Searle
Dr Kathy Seddon
Paul Sellers
Hopi Sen
Mina Silva
Rohan Silva
Melanie Sinclair
Clifford Singer
Greg Slay

Martin Small
Ashley Smith
Graham Smith
Nicola Smith
Diana Soffa
Libor Špaček, PhD
Jon Spain
Jeannine St. Amand
Paul Stanley
Simon Stanley
Wiard Sterk
Lee Strafford
Tony Stroud
Mark Poul Stubbs
Andrea Sukhnandan
Laura Sukhnandan
Niclas Svahnström
Kirsten Sydendal
Hanns Tappen
Matthew Taylor
Roger Taylor
Chris Tchen
Sarah Thelwall
James Thompson
Julian Thompson
James Thorp
Jonathan Todd
Jon Tollit
Paul Tompsett
Julia Tratt
Dimitar Trifonov

Robin Tuddenham
Nancy Turner
Peter C Turner
Julia Unwin
Nicole Vanderbilt
Anne Verrept
Luciano Volpe
Paul Walsh
Elly Ward
Adam Warn
Chet Warzynski
Kumari Amy Weaver
Emily Weiner
Rich A West
Stian Westlake
Jody Wetton
Alex White
Dale White
Edward Whitelaw
David Wilcox
Dyfan Williams
Richard Williams
Richard Wilson
Ann Winter
Dar Wolnik
Iain Wood
James K Wood
Clare Woodcraft-Scott
Scott 'Woolfie' Woolf
Antonia Wrigley